18

AMERICA'S FIRST AIR WAR

THE UNITED STATES ARMY, NAVAL AND MARINE AIR SERVICES IN THE FIRST WORLD WAR

TERRY C. TREADWELL

Airlife
England

Copyright © 2000 Terry C. Treadwell

First published in the UK in 2000
by Airlife Publishing Ltd

British Library Cataloguing-in-Publication Data
    A catalogue record for this book
    is available from the British Library

ISBN 1 84037 113 7

Typeset by Servis Filmsetting Ltd, Manchester
Printed in England by Butler & Tanner Ltd, London and Frome.

Airlife Publishing Ltd
101 Longden Road, Shrewsbury, SY3 9EB, England
E-mail: airlife@airlifebooks.com
Website: www.airlifebooks.com

For I dipt into the future, far as human eye could see,
Saw the Vision of the world, and all the wonder that would be;
Saw the heavens fill with commerce, argosies of magic sails,
Pilots of the purple twilight, dropping down with costly bales;
Heard the heavens fill with shouting, and there rain'd a ghastly dew
From the nations' airy navies grappling in the central blue

'Locksley Hall', Tennyson

Preface

This book is about the part played by the United States Army, Naval and Marine Air Services in the First World War. It is not a definitive work, but an essentially pictorial book, including 140 photographs, some of which have rarely been seen before.

The American contribution to the First World War has always been regarded as minimal, basically because of the short period of time that they were involved. But it has to be said, minimal or not, their involvement helped to tip the balance of power in favour of the Allies. Large numbers of American infantrymen died in the fiercely fought battles that brought the war to an end. Many of their pilots and observers were slaughtered by a battle-hardened enemy, even before they had experienced any part of the war.

The first part of this book covers the early development of the use of the balloon in warfare. It then progresses to the development of the USAS and USNAS and their first use of aircraft in a combat situation, when General Pershing tracked the Mexican bandit and revolutionary Pancho Villa across Mexico during the Mexican revolution, albeit with little success. Also covered is the incident off Veracruz when an aircraft of the USNAS came under rifle fire and was the first American aircraft to be hit by gunfire during a conflict.

Covered in some detail are the main reasons why the United States entered the war and the violations by Germany that exacerbated the situation. With the advent of the First War, the first American adventurers went to France to fight voluntarily with the *Escadrille Lafayette*, Royal Flying Corps, Royal Naval Air Service and the French Air Service, before joining the newly created United States Air Service. Also covered is the founding of the US Army and Navy air units through the Signal Corps, National Guard, the First Yale Unit and the Governor's Island Training School. By the time of the Armistice the numbers of American pilots and ground crews who went to fight the air war in France had risen from 4,000 to over 300,000.

The US Navy and Marine Corps pilots also fought alongside their compatriots in the army with equal determination, yet very little is ever said about this. This book hopes to redress the balance in some small way and give an insight into the early development of what was to become one of the most powerful air forces in the world. The book also deals with some of the personalities that emerged from the war: the loners, the aces, and the mavericks. Also not forgotten are the ordinary young pilots and observers who saw barely any of the fighting before dying before the guns of the battle-hardened German pilots.

The last section of the book contains copies of original PoW escape reports from USAS pilots and observers, which give a detailed insight into the conditions under which these and other Allied soldiers were kept imprisoned.

All photographs are from my own collection, except where indicated.

Terry Treadwell

First Army Wright type 'C' airplane in the Philippines at Fort McKinley in February 1912. L–R: Lt H.A. Darque, Lt C.G. Chapman, Lt F.P. Lahm (pilot), Lt P.C. Rich and Sgt V.L. Burge.

Contents

Chapter 1

In the Beginning

The birth of the United States Army Air Service was heralded by the establishment of a balloon section by the Signal Corps in 1891. The Franco-Prussian War in 1870 had brought the balloon into the forefront of military use in Europe when, during the conflict, the city of Paris was cut off from the outside world by an encirclement of German forces. Extensive use was made of balloons to carry letters and dispatches out of Paris and stay in contact with the rest of France and its army. These letters and dispatches were mostly carried by night to prevent the balloons being attacked by the Germans. So successful were these flights that at the end of the war officers from the various European countries were sent for training at the French Aérostation, in order to gain specialist knowledge so that they too could develop their own military balloon companies.

Balloons had been used earlier, during the American Civil War, in 1861 when a number of experienced balloonists, among them Thadeus Lowe, John LaMountain and John Wise, offered their services to the Union Army. The first successful recorded observation was made during the Cape Hatteras Expedition in August 1861, when John LaMountain discovered concealed Confederate camps during an ascent above the Cape. This information was of great interest to the expedition's commander, General Butler, who was able to destroy the camps with limited casualties to his men.

In Washington, President Abraham Lincoln took an interest in the wartime use of the balloon and summoned Thadeus Lowe to him. Lowe talked with the President, hoping to convince him of the use of a balloon corps. Then, on 24 July 1861, Lowe was asked to make an observation flight from Fort Corcoran to allay fears of a Confederate force marching on the capital. This was done successfully, and Lowe was able to report that there was no large Confederate force anywhere near. Then, just before the Battle of Manassas, President Lincoln sent Lowe to General Winfield Scott, Commander-in-Chief of the Union Armies, to see if the balloon would be of use as an observation platform. It soon became clear, however, that General Scott was not one of those inclined towards the use of the balloon and there is no record of any flights taking place before or during the battle. The Union Army took a terrible beating and both sides lost large numbers of troops.

Lowe was sent for again by Lincoln to ask whether or not he thought the balloon might have made a significant difference to the outcome. Lowe, of course, said that in his opinion the balloon may have been able to give the ground forces information on the movements of the Confederate forces, but they would never know. President Lincoln sent Lowe to meet again with General Scott, this time with a personal message card: 'Will Lieut. Gen. Scott please see Professor Lowe once more about his balloon? A. Lincoln, 25 July 1861.' On three separate occasions Scott refused to see Lowe for a variety of reasons. Angry, Lowe went to see Lincoln, who personally escorted Lowe to Scott's headquarters. On being confronted by the President, Scott agreed to look very seriously at the formation of a balloon corps.

Thadeus Lowe was offered a position with a salary of thirty dollars a day for every day his balloon was used, but Lowe wanted more. He wanted a regular salary and a position of military aeronaut, with a commission to build a balloon. With support from various quarters, this was agreed, and Lowe set about building his balloon, named the *Union*. The balloon was of 25,000 cubic feet and made of India silk with linen cordage and rigging. The first balloon corps had its first balloon.

The usefulness of this new balloon was highlighted when on 24 September 1862, at Falls Church, Virginia, Thadeus S. Lowe directed Federal artillery onto the Confederate Army from a tethered balloon by means of a crude telegraph system (flags). The use of the balloon during this particular battle enhanced the accuracy of the cannon fire to a large degree and played a significant part in the outcome, and again it also served well as an observation platform. During the crossing of the Rappahannock River on 11 December 1862, a balloon was used to great effect, enabling the Federal Army to cross unhindered. The service developed slowly, however, and although a number of balloons were used, only nine other aeronauts were ever employed and none was given military status; the army, although accepting their services, refused to accept them into their ranks, Lowe being the one exception,

Professor Lowe's balloon being inflated.

Professor Lowe launching his observation balloon Intrepid, *during the American Civil War.*

Professor Lowe in his observation balloon being launched.

highlighting the barrier between the old ways and progress.

Moving the balloons to different places started to become a problem. As a large number of the battles appeared to be happening around the Potomac River area, it was decided to operate observation stations along its banks. Supplying the various stations was carried out by coal barge, which was towed by a tug, or occasionally moved by means of paddles or oars. The balloon corps made full use of this barge to transport their balloon and equipment to the various areas of war, thus creating the first 'aircraft carrier'.

Over the following years, the balloon corps was shuttled between various departments of the army – the Topographical Engineers, the Quartermaster and the Corps of Engineers –

where, after the war, it faded into obscurity. Change was not a thing the army liked, and although somewhat grudgingly, it accepted that the balloon had played its part in the war. But the diehards were not convinced that the balloon had a future in the military.

It was not until 1891 that radical new thoughts started to open the minds of the United States military hierarchy. The Americans up to this point had shown little or no interest in the balloon, even though it had proved its worth during the Civil War. One balloon, however, was used by the Americans in Cuba during the Spanish-American War of 1898. The whole episode was a débâcle. The troops arrived on 22 June 1898, but the balloon corps did not arrive until 28 June. The equipment for the balloon was contained in seven wagons, and when it was finally unpacked, it was found that the varnish had softened to the degree that nearly all the panels of the balloon had stuck together. Only after extensive repairs had been made and the balloon inflated was it possible to make any ascents. Even so, there was a great deal of trepidation on the part of the observers as to whether or not the repairs would hold. Three ascents were made altogether, but only a matter of days later the balloon was totally destroyed by enemy gunfire. Interest in the balloon waned rapidly, and its development was put on hold.

But while the rest of the world was still concentrating on the use of balloons, in America, two brothers, Wilbur and Orville Wright, were about to turn the world of aviation upside down. On 17 December 1903, at Kitty Hawk, North Carolina, the two brothers carried out the first powered flight of an aeroplane. This almost immediately relegated the balloon into second place and opened the way for a new concept of aerial transport, be it for war or peaceful purposes.

Within the United States military however, the balloon was now, somewhat belatedly, starting to attract attention again as an observation platform and some money was found by Congress for balloon development. A small balloon facility was opened at Fort Myers, Virginia, to look into the possibilities of the use of the balloon within the military. After a great deal of study by a group of dedicated enthusiasts, including Major Frank Lahm – the first American to receive a balloonist's licence – and Captain Charles De F. Chandler, an aeronautical division was created in 1907, in the Office of Chief Signal Officer in Washington. One year later, the near-defunct balloon facility at Fort Myers was transferred to Fort Omaha, Nebraska and a balloon school opened under the command of newly promoted Major Charles De F. Chandler. The location of the school was perfect: there was no smoke from nearby cities or towns to pollute the air and it was situated on a large plain giving the

students and instructors a superb panoramic view. It was also relatively close to the General Staff College at Fort Leavenworth, Kansas, where officers could be billeted while attending courses at the balloon school.

In May 1917 the school was put under the command of Major Frank Lahm (Major Chandler having been posted to Washington to the Office of the Chief Signal Officer), but in September, Lahm, together with Major Chandler, was sent to France to observe balloon training and combat deployment on the Western Front. During this period Lahm and Chandler carried out a number of missions themselves, taking the observation balloons to heights of over 1,500 feet. They had watched helplessly from the ground on a number of other occasions when German fighter aircraft attacked defenceless balloons, highlighting the dangers that the balloonists and their ground crews faced every time they ascended to carry out reconnaissance missions.

The French had developed the Caquot observation balloon, named after its inventor, French Army captain Alfred Caquot. The balloon was a near oval shape with fins on the tail that enabled it to attain excellent stability at heights of up to 4,000 feet and in winds of 60mph, thus creating an extremely stable observation platform. Nicknamed the 'Elephant' by its ground crews, the Caquot balloon was made of a very strong rubberised fabric which resisted a certain amount of sustained machine-gun fire. The only drawback was that it had to be inflated by means of highly inflammable hydrogen gas which, if ignited, would turn the balloon almost instantaneously into a raging inferno.

In the meantime, the development of the aircraft in the United States had continued its slow, plodding progress after the initial excitement, but speculation as to what this new machine could offer had disappeared, and it was left to the Europeans to look upon this new invention as a weapon of war. In 1907, the President of the American Aero Club, Cortland Bishop, sent an article from the

Eugene Ely's Curtiss Pusher aboard the light cruiser USS Birmingham *in the Norfolk Navy Yard. The aircraft is being serviced prior to leaving on its historic flight.*

magazine *Scientific American*, to President Teddy Roosevelt. Roosevelt was impressed and asked the US War department to look into the use of the aircraft as a military machine. America had given the world the first aeroplane and then, to all intents and purposes, appeared to have abandoned it as a serious military machine. They had watched with great interest the development of the air forces of the European nations as they fought over the skies of Europe, but they themselves had done very little to form their own air force. However,

there were, fortunately, a number of people in America who had the foresight to see that the aeroplane had an important part to play as a leading weapon of war and took measures to see that their country would not be left behind.

Interest in the world of naval aviation was nurtured by Captain Washington Irving Chambers, later regarded by many as the father of US naval aviation. Chambers had attended the international air meet at Belmont Park, New York during October 1910 and had met designers, manufacturers and pilots. So

Eugene Ely in his Curtiss Pusher about to make the world's first landing on a ship, the USS Pennsylvania. *Note the sandbag-weighted ropes stretched across the deck.*

impressed was he that he persuaded the Department of the Navy to part with $25,000 for the acquisition of two aircraft. Chambers wasted no time in getting things moving, and one month later, on 14 November 1910, aided by a civilian pilot by the name of Eugene Ely from the Curtiss plant, he carried out the first ship-to-shore flight. A specially built structure was assembled over the forecastle of the scout cruiser USS *Birmingham* (CL-2), which was anchored off Old Point Comfort, Virginia. Eugene Ely, in a 50hp Curtiss Pusher, opened the throttle of the engine and roared down the 83-foot-long, 24-foot-wide platform with a downward slope of 5 degrees, and into the air. The aircraft dropped momentarily, the propeller just clipping the water, and then climbed into the air. Ely headed the aircraft for the shore and made a safe landing.

Chambers had proved that the aircraft was a

viable investment, but he still had to convince the sceptics. While these doubters were still pondering over the flight, Chambers arranged for a second demonstration, only this time the aircraft was to land on the deck of a ship then take off again. On 18 January 1911, Ely took off from a field at Tanforan, just south of San Francisco, and headed for the armoured cruiser USS *Pennsylvania* (ACR-4). The ship, which was anchored off Hunter's Point in San Francisco Bay, had had a somewhat larger platform built over its stern. Like the platform built on the USS *Birmingham* it had a five-degree-slope, but in addition there were twenty-two ropes stretched across the deck, each weighted down with 50lb-sandbags. The idea was that the three pairs of steel hooks fitted on the undercarriage bar beneath the aircraft would catch the ropes and bring the aircraft to a halt. The demonstration was a complete success, but it was still to take a number of years and more experiments before the sceptics were completely convinced.

The navy was also the first American military force to display the aircraft's practical use. On 6 October 1912, Lt John H. Towers, flying a Curtiss A-2 floatplane, took off from the water at Annapolis and remained in the air for six hours, ten minutes and thirty-five seconds, emphasising the use of the aircraft for reconnaissance purposes.

In January 1914, the United States Navy opened its first Naval Air Station at Pensacola, Florida. The training of pilots and ground crews was informal, had no sense of discipline or purpose and comprised mainly graduates from Annapolis. The curriculum was unstructured at the time, only covering the technical side of aviation and for some unknown reason omitting fundamental navigation and seamanship. It has to be remembered that aviation was something completely new, and there were very few skilled personnel to teach students. Everyone was on a learning curve, including the instructors. Slowly but surely, though, the curriculum was tightened up and the standard of instruction improved.

Eugene Ely with Captain Charles F. Pond of the USS Pennsylvania *after his historic landing aboard the USS* Pennsylvania. *Note the inflated bicycle tyres around Ely's body in case he had to ditch in the sea.*

The first American Army squadron, Aero Squadron No. 1, comprising eight aircraft made up of Curtiss JN-3s and R-4s, had been put together in 1913 when it was feared that there was going to be a revolution in Mexico. The pilots – Lts Eric L. Ellington, Loren H. Call, Charles J. Boeha, Fred Seydel, Ralph Jones, H.M. Kelly, Moss L. Love, Townsend F. Dove and J.C. Morrow – had been taken from the aviation school at San Diego. The squadron was formed at Columbus, New Mexico and put on standby in case they were needed, but when the revolution failed to materialise the pilots were returned to the school at San Diego. This was not the first time aircraft had been considered for use in a military capacity against the Mexicans. The first recorded use was in February 1911, when a US government pilot carried out a reconnaissance flight over the rebel forces at Ciudad Juárez, but did not carry out any aggressive action.

As part of Fleet manoeuvres in January 1913, the United States Navy set up an aviation camp on Fisherman's Point, Guantanamo Bay, Cuba. The aircraft flew scouting missions and carried out spotting sorties looking for mines and submerged submarines. So successful were they that a great deal of interest was generated within the navy towards this new addition to their operational capabilities, but unfortunately the major and influential interest was missing.

Then, in April 1914, the prospect of a revolution in Mexico reared its head again, only this time it was the US Navy who were involved. The first message that mobilised the naval aviation section into action was sent to Pensacola on Sunday, 19 April 1914. It was sent to Captain William Sims while he was having lunch aboard the aeronautical training ship, the cruiser USS *Birmingham,* with the captain of the ship, Lieutenant-Commander Henry 'Rum' Mustin. The message read:

DIRECT COMMANDING OFFICER AERONAUTIC STATION REPORT YOU FOR SERVICE ONE AEROPLANE SECTION CONSISTING TWO FLYING BOATS OR HYDROAEROPLANES ONE SPARE BOAT OR PONTOON TWO SPARE MOTORS TWO HANGARS TENTAGE FOR PERSONAL AND OTHER NECESSARY SPARES AND OUTFITS. LIEUTENANT TOWERS IN CHARGE WITH LIEUTENANT SMITH AND ENSIGN CHEVALIER AND TEN MECHANICIENS.

Lt-Cdr Mustin went on deck to inspect the facilities required for such a mission. The USS *Birmingham* had been in the public eye on 14 November 1910 when Eugene Ely had flown a Curtiss Pusher from her deck, only this time aircraft were going to have to fly from her deck under battle conditions. If successful, it would be a great boost for naval aviation; if not, it could sound the death knell. After his initial inspection, Mustin realised that the ship had no facilities for hoisting the aircraft into or out of the water. Lowering booms were quickly installed on the mainmast to serve as derricks.

The unstable situation in Mexico suddenly reached a critical point: a message was received in Washington that a German merchant ship was to dock on 21 April at Veracruz, with a cargo of weapons and ammunition for General Victoria Huerta's troops. The USS *Birmingham,* with an aviation detachment aboard comprising three pilots, three aircraft and twelve enlisted men under the command of Lt John H. Towers, was immediately dispatched to join the Atlantic Fleet forces operating off the coast to Tampico. Meanwhile, the USS *Mississippi,* under the command of Rear-Admiral Frank Jack Fletcher, with a second aviation detachment aboard, was dispatched to assist in the military operations at Veracruz. On 21 April 1914, the Fleet landing force lost nineteen men to snipers from the revolutionary army when they attempted to seize Veracruz.

The city itself was a contrast of extremes. The pastel-painted buildings with their green and pink balconies set against the background of deep azure-blue skies presented a beautiful sight, but the vast majority of the city had no sanitation, disease was rampant and the whole area reeked repulsively of rotting refuse and human waste. This cesspit of a city was what the US Navy and Marines were about to try to take.

The USS *Mississippi* launched its first observation flight, an AB-3 flying boat flown by Lt (jg) P.N.L. Bellinger,[*] over the harbour of Veracruz to search for mines. Two days later a second flight was made, again by Bellinger but this time accompanied by an observer, Ensign W.D. LaMont, to photograph the harbour. On 2 May 1914, the USS *Mississippi* launched a third flight, this time in a Curtiss C-3 (AH-3) floatplane, to search for enemy troops reported near Tejar. After flying for over fifty minutes they returned to the ship having seen nothing but American Army troops, but what they had done was to record the first American aerial mission under military conflict conditions. Four days later, on 6 May 1914, Bellinger, with Lt (jg) Saufley[**] as observer, flew a reconnaissance flight over enemy positions near Veracruz. Their aircraft was hit by rifle fire

---

[*]Bellinger later commanded one of the four NC aircraft, the NC-1, in the US Navy's successful attempt to fly the Atlantic, although only one, the NC-4, was to complete the trip. Bellinger also became an admiral in World War Two.

[**]Saufley was to lose his life on 9 June 1916 when his AH-9 aircraft crashed into the sea off Santa Rosa Island, Pensacola. It happened during an endurance flight after the aircraft had been in the air for eight hours and fifty-one minutes. The cause is not known, but was possibly engine failure.

USN aircraft over Vera Cruz during the 1914 expedition. In the background, just visible, are US Naval ships at anchor in the harbour.

from the 'invisible' enemy – the first marks of combat on a US naval aircraft. Over the next few days the two men carried out several more observation flights over the town, more as a show of strength than a serious threat, but fortunately without any further incidents. The flights were merely token gestures in support of the 'bluejackets', who were already in the town mopping up resistance.

An aviation camp was set up on the beach and the work of scouting the area continued. After flying a number of missions during the next month with no results, the number of flights was reduced to one a day. The crews of the aircraft were looking for ghosts, and they knew it. The Navy felt that it was a waste of time and effort to continue, but were told that they would have to stay until the Army was able to get some of their Air Service aircraft there. No. 1 Aero Squadron had been dispatched to aid the Navy, but by the time they reached Fort Crocket, near Galveston, Texas, the incident in Mexico was over and the squadron, together with its uncrated aircraft,

Pancho Villa on the left with machine-gun, with one of his lieutenants.

Venustiano Carranza – President of Mexico in 1916.

returned to San Diego. This in reality made a nonsense of the attempt to provide air support for ground troops, and highlighted the lack of commitment at the time by the American government to the future of air power. However, it did spur on the manufacturers of aircraft (only twelve of the manufacturers were deemed capable of producing what could loosely be called military aircraft at that time) into

looking at the problem with serious intent. Four hundred aircraft were produced during 1916, and not one could be considered to be a pure military aircraft.

Then, early in 1916, one Doroteo Arango, also known as Francisco Pancho Villa, appeared on the scene in Mexico. Pancho Villa was born in 1877 in the small village of Rio Grande in the Mexican state of Durango. He began his career as a bandit in northern Mexico in the early 1900s, rustling cattle and holding up stagecoaches. By 1910 he had turned his talents into fighting a revolution, and was largely responsible for the overthrow of Porfirio Diaz; he also became the sworn enemy of General Venustiano Carranza, head of the de facto constitutionalist government of Mexico.

Uneducated as he was, Pancho Villa could see that there was a place for aircraft as an observation platform and possibly a bomber. With this in mind he invited an American by the name of Edwin C. Parsons to come to Mexico and train some of his officers to fly. Parsons, the son of a wealthy businessman from Springfield, Massachusetts, had been taught to fly by the aircraft manufacturer Glen L. Martin and had been working in the film industry as a stuntman/pilot, among other things. At the beginning of 1913, together with a friend of his, another pilot by the name of Jean de Villa, Parsons went to Mexico to train some of Pancho Villa's officers. For nearly a year the two Americans desperately tried to train the officers, but to no avail. The major problem facing the two instructors was the simple act of getting the potential aviators just to set one foot inside the cockpit. They were terrified of the machine, and only one of the officers could be said to have grasped the rudiments of flying. After a number of accidents, which angered Pancho Villa, mainly because he couldn't understand why they happened, the two Americans decided to leave. Their decision was hastened when a German agent operating in Mexico warned the two men to leave, as Pancho Villa was about to embark on a dangerous game that would involve the United States. The two men headed for the border under the pretence of getting spares for the aircraft and never returned. It was while in Philadelphia some months later that Parsons heard of the formation of the *Escadrille Américaine*, and so headed for France.

Later in 1914, Pancho Villa joined forces with Emiliano Zapata and marched into Mexico City, forcing General Carranza to flee to Veracruz. There, Carranza joined forces with Alvaro Obregon, and nine months later retook the capital. The revolutionaries had in fact used an aeroplane piloted by a Mexican officer, Captain Gustavo Salinas, in an attack on General Victoria Huerta's troops in April 1914. He had dropped a number of crude bombs on Huerta's troops, none of which

Emiliano Zapata.

San Antonio Express.

VOLUME LI— NO. 331.   SAN ANTONIO, TEXAS, SUNDAY MORNING, NOVEMBER 26, 1916.—SEVENTY-EIGHT PAGES.   ESTABLISHED 1865.

TEUTONS CROSS ALT RIVER, LAST BARRIER IN THEIR DRIVE ON BUCHAREST

Von Mackensen Advances From Southwest to Effect Junction With Falkenhayn's Forces.

ROUMANIA MAY SEEK PEACE

Serious Consideration Given to Food Embargo Question by President

FRENCH COMPLAIN OF BEING FORCED CARRY WAR BRUNT

ALARM SOUNDED BY DEPUTIES AGAINST EXHAUSTION OF NATION.

CLASS OF '18 MUSTERED IN

CLOSER CHECK TO BE KEPT ON MEXICAN PLOTTERS IN THE U.S.

Pledge to Watch Anti-Carrancistas on This Side of Border Given in Addition to Protocol.

DOUBT CARRANZA'S COURSE

REPULSING MURGUIA, VILLA SHIFTS ATTACK

Keeps Reinforcements From Trevino and Cuts Wires Leading to Juarez

Over Indian Trail Three Centuries Old, Four Americans Flee Villa and Are Saved

The four American mining men who fled Parral at Villa's approach and reached the border at Nogales in record time after declaring southwest to Culiacan on the west coast of Mexico. Reading from left to right: A. W. Morris of Los Angeles, former Consul Daughtery of Nogales, who maintained the refugees: Bernard McDonald, L. Webb and Z. G. Hawkins of El Paso.

BELIEVE CAPITAL STILL IS HELD BY CARRANZA ARMY

Reports of Cannonading Give Hope to Juarez Officials That Chihuahua Is Holding Out.

FIGHTING BEGINS AT DAWN

ASSERTS UNIONISM WILL KEEP MEXICO AND U.S. AT PEACE

FRATERNAL DELEGATE FROM YUCATAN ADDRESSES LABOR DELEGATE.

GOMPERS IS RE-ELECTED

BREAK RECORD IN RACE FOR LIVES

Go From Parral to Culiacan in Eight Days.

Reach Nogales and Make Light of Hardships—Fate of Companions Left Behind Still a Mystery

GUARD TO REMAIN UNTIL PERSHING'S MEN ARE RECALLED

REDISPOSITION OF REGULARS AFTER PROTOCOL IS RATIFIED, IS PLANNED.

TO HELP MEXICO GET LOAN

More Than 125,000 See the Great Football Classics of the Season; Yale and West Point Winners

YALE BOYS TAKE HARD GAME FROM HARVARD, 6 TO 3

OLD ELI WINS BY PLAYING STEADY, CONSISTENT FOOTBALL

ARMY TRIUMPHS IN SPECTACULAR GAME OVER MIDDIES, 15-7

NAVY FIGHTS GAMELY UNTIL THE FINAL WHISTLE, BUT IS OUTCLASSED

GREEKS YIELD TO ALLIED ULTIMATUM; SURRENDER ARMS

CABINET AGAIN ABOUT TO RESIGN—PROVISIONAL GOVERNMENT DECLARES WAR

TODAY'S EXPRESS 78 PAGES

Consisting of 5 Sections.

News Section: 28 pages.
Society Section: 16 pages.
Auto and Sport Section: 14 pages.
Comic Section: 4 pages.
Real Estate and Classified Section: 20 pages.

72,000,000 Eggs Held by "Egg King" Are Seized in Raid to Reduce Living Cost

1st Aero Squadron. L–R: Lt Clinton W. Russell, Lt John B. Brooks, Unknown, Captain Benjamin D. Foulis.

caused any serious damage, while they were defending the port city of Mazathan. In September 1915, Pancho Villa then attacked Carranza's garrison at Agua Prieta and suffered heavy losses, his army of followers decimated. This attack was repulsed by Carranza using aeroplanes flown by American mercenary pilots. Among these pilots was Didier Masson, a Frenchman, who was later to become a member of the legendary *Lafayette Escadrille*. Masson at one time even tried dropping a can of dynamite down the funnel of Huerta's one and only gunboat, the first attempt by an American to carry out an aerial bombing attack, but it was woefully unsuccessful. So Mexico can lay claim to being one of the first countries to use aircraft in warfare, even though their pilots in the main were mercenaries.

Although this was a Mexican problem, the garrison at Agua Prieta was on the US–Mexican border a few miles from Douglas, Arizona. So concerned were the residents of the town that the governor of Arizona asked the US Army for help, and they dispatched the 1st Aero Squadron to San Antonio, Texas. Pancho Villa in the meantime had fled back north to regroup and reassess his situation. On 11 January 1916, Pancho Villa and a heavily armed army of horsemen stopped a train not far from the town of Chihuahua and murdered nineteen Americans

Lt Carelton G. Chapman's aircraft in the barren landscape of Mexico during the Mexican Punitive Campaign.

who were on board. Carranza, now recognised by the Americans as the legitimate ruler of Mexico, made a determined effort to finish Pancho Villa and went after him with a vengeance. The fact that America officially recognised Carranza as President of Mexico so incensed Pancho Villa that on 9 March 1916, with between 500 and 1,000 men (the exact figure is not known), he attacked the town of Columbus, New Mexico, burning homes, killing eighteen American soldiers and civilians and wounding seven others. This was the first foreign invasion of the United States since 1812 – and the last. Pancho Villa was chased back across the border by the United States Cavalry. On 10 March 1916, President Woodrow Wilson ordered General John 'Black Jack' Pershing to mount a punitive expedition of some 10,000 troops and the 1st Aero Squadron into Mexico to find and destroy Pancho Villa. For over a year the Army and 1st Aero Squadron pursued Pancho Villa through deserts and over mountains, but to no avail.

During General Pershing's expedition, No. 1

Curtiss JN–3s at Columbus, New Mexico.

Lt Carelton G. Chapman, USAAS, taxying for take-off in Mexico during the Mexican Punitive Campaign.

Aero Squadron, under the command of Captain Benjamin D. Foulis, had been assigned to provide some form of air support. As gun platforms the aircraft were totally ineffective, but in the area of communications, reconnaissance and courier work they were vital. Because of the vast distances and the number of troop columns that were spread out across the terrain, the only way Pershing could keep in touch with his commanders was by using aircraft. Radios at the time were ineffective and low-powered, and the mountains created static which made transmissions almost inaudible. The mountains protecting the Casa Grandes of Mexico were only 12,000 feet high, but because of the hot, dry air the aircraft from No. 1 Aero Squadron were unable to fly over them. In fact most of the time they had great difficulty staying airborne, even close to the ground, but despite all these difficulties the Squadron managed to prove that the aircraft did have its place in war, although not to General Pershing's full satisfaction.

The expedition lasted just over a year, and it was not only the soldiers and airmen who took a beating from the torturous heat and terrain; the aircrafts' wings and undercarriage suffered badly from the sagebrush and heavy landings on the rough ground. The aircraft and their pilots returned to their base at Columbus, New Mexico, to reflect on what they had learned. The then Secretary of the Navy, Josephus Daniels, announced to Congress that the point had been reached 'where aircraft must form a large part of our forces for offensive and defensive operations'.

Pancho Villa was never caught. He was later assassinated, together with his secretary, Colonel Miguel Trillo, and three of his bodyguards, at 0800 on 11 July 1923, in Guadalupe, a suburb of Hidalgo del Parral, Chihuahua, Mexico, while driving in his Dodge automobile through the town towards his ranch at Canutillo. His assassin, Jesús Salas Barrazas, said on his release, after serving only six months of a twenty-year sentence, 'I'm not a murderer, I rid humanity of a monster.'

New York Tribune

900 Die as Lusitania Goes to Bottom; 400 Americans on Board Torpedoed Ship; Washington Stirred as When Maine Sank

CAPITAL AROUSED, SITUATION GRAVEST YET FACED IN WAR

Washington Determined That Germany Shall Not Be Allowed to Shirk Responsibility for Deaths.

GREATLY FEARS LOSS OF AMERICANS

President Shows Nervousness as Bulletins of Disaster Come In. Strongest Protest Yet Made Planned Even if No U.S. Citizens Were Lost.

Washington, May 7.—The news of the heavy loss of life on the Lusitania stirred Washington as it has not been stirred since the sinking of the Maine. The earlier reports that both passengers and crew had been landed safely had quieted apprehension of an immediate crisis in the relations of the United States and Germany. But when it became clear that Americans—undoubtedly a considerable number of them—were to be counted among the victims of German measures at sea the full significance of the tragedy difficulties struck home.

President Wilson made little effort to conceal his feelings. At New York tonight the President received the following dispatch from the United States Consul at Cork:

"Lusitania sunk at 2:30 o'clock. Probably many survivors. Rescue work proceeding favorably. Shall I send you list of survivors."

Mr. Wilson as he read it he put on his hat and walked out of the White House without the knowledge of the Secret Service men who were guarding him. The President walked up Sixteenth Street to Corcoran street, crossed over to Fifteenth Street and back to the White House, where he went into his study to await further information. He had to form over in his mind the message that it is expected he will send to the German Foreign Office as soon as all the details of the disaster are known.

Cabinet To Be Called Together

The President will probably call the whole Cabinet together to discuss the questions of the policy which the government may take.

LONDON SEES VITAL QUESTION FOR U. S.

America is 'Bound to Defend Lives of Its Subjects,' Declares 'Daily News.'

London, May 8.—The "Daily Chronicle" says editorially to-day:

"To destroy by deliberate aim one of the great floating castles which across the Atlantic without something like 2,000 lives in their keeping, is to attempt, in cold blood such a massacre as a foot-combatants as even the most ferocious conquerors have seldom perpetrated save in fear.

GERMANS TOAST 'VICTORY' AMID 'HOCHS' IN CAFES

Steins Clink as Celebrators Predict Downfall of Britain's Sea Power.

OFFICERS GAY IN CLUBHOUSE

Restaurants Thronged and Entire Families Out to Cheer Kaiser and His Submarines.

"Deutschland, Deutschland, über Alles" resounded last night wherever Germans met to discuss and to toast "the day" which, in their mind, ended the fate of British world dominion on the sea. In the fashionable German Club, headquarters of the Teutonic élite and camping ground of German military officers unable to join their métier, the sinking of the Lusitania was the principal topic of animated conversation. Everything else was forgotten in the glow of news at Britain, the "arch enemy," through the torpedoing of the Lusitania.

U. S. OWES IT TO SELF-RESPECT TO ACT, SAYS ROOSEVELT; 'PIRACY ON VAST SCALE.'

Syracuse, May 7.—After the appalling details of the Lusitania disaster had been told to Colonel Roosevelt late to-night he said: "It seems inconceivable that we should refrain from taking action on this matter, for we owe it not only to humanity but to our own national self-respect.

"This represents not merely piracy, but piracy on a vaster scale of murder than any old-time pirate ever practiced. This is the warfare which destroyed Louvain and Dinant and hundreds of men, women and children in Belgium, warfare to innocent men, women and children travelling on the ocean, to our own fellow country men and country women who are among the sufferers."

ACT OF BARBARITY, SAYS F. R. COUDERT

Lawyer Insists Sinking of the Lusitania Is Without Justification.

"An act of barbarity without justification," was the expression of Frederic R. Coudert, of the law firm of Coudert Brothers, in referring to the torpedoing of the Lusitania.

"I make that statement on the supposition that lives of citizens of the United States, a neutral nation, were destroyed by the sinking of the ship."

MANY NOTED NEW YORKERS ON LUSITANIA

Alfred G. Vanderbilt Was on Way to England on Business Trip.

N. J. REPRESENTED ON FIRST CABIN LIST

Charles Frohman, Lindon Bates, Jr., Charles Klein and Justus Miles Forman Aboard.

As usual, a large proportion of the Lusitania first cabin list was composed of New Yorkers.

Alfred G. Vanderbilt was necessarily a prominent figure among the passengers. His business connection was, the many others explained when he heard the first rumors about the Cunarder's fate, Captain George C. Day and Commander F. L. Sawyer, both United States naval officers, who are working with Mr. Vanderbilt on the plans for the reception of the Atlantic fleet, were incredulous, too. But when Mr. Vanderbilt learned through The Tribune that the news had been confirmed, he asked the newspapers for his outside bulletin.

Mrs. Brother Alfred expected to be quite for four or five hours of his dred and five passengers. Each of the war, Mr. Vanderbilt would have accompanied her husband on the Lusitania.

PASSENGERS WERE AT LUNCHEON

The tug Stormcock returned to Queenstown, bringing about one hundred and fifty survivors, principally passengers, among whom were many women, several of the crew and one steward.

Describing the experience of the Lusitania, the steward said: "The passengers were at luncheon, when a submarine came and fired two torpedoes, which struck the Lusitania on the starboard side, one forward and the other in the engine room. They caused terrific explosions.

"Captain Turner immediately ordered the boats out. The ship began to list heavily immediately.

"Ten boats were put into the water, and between four hundred and five hundred passengers entered them. The boat in which I was approached the land with three other boats, and were picked up shortly after 4 o'clock by the Stormcock bravely.

WENT DOWN BY BOW.

"There were only fifteen minutes from the time the ship was struck until she foundered, going down bow foremost. It was a dreadful sight."

More dispatches brought word that the hotel and lodging houses are being canvassed in an effort to obtain more or less authoritative lists of the survivors.

One of the first persons landed from the ship by a boat which reached Kinsale Head was General H. B. Lassetter, late commander of an Australian Light Horse Brigade. His wife and son were returning from a trip to Los Angeles. George A. Kessler, the New York wine agent, and Mrs. J. T. Smith, of Braceville, Ohio, were also reported among the saved.

The Admiralty gave out the official news about midnight that the attack was made in broad daylight and with absolutely no warning.

A Queenstown dispatch to "The Daily Chronicle" says that seven torpedoes were discharged from the German craft and that one of them struck the Lusitania amidships.

There is no question in any one's mind here that it was a submarine which caused the disaster. There is information at hand

Dying and Injured Brought in with Other Survivors to Queenstown—Some Landed at Kinsale and Clonakilty.

TWO TORPEDOES FIRED, SAYS STEWARD

Attack Made About Eight Miles from Irish Coast in Broad Daylight and in Fine Weather—Survivor Tells of Bravery of Cunard Officers.

London, May 8, 3 a. m.—At least 900 lives were lost when the Lusitania was torpedoed without warning in broad daylight yesterday afternoon by a German submarine, according to estimates by survivors. The estimate of First Officer Jones puts the total nearer 1,500.

Of the dead more than two hundred are supposed to be Americans, as it is believed there were about 400 on board.

A dispatch from Queenstown sent out at midnight says:

"Up to the present 520 passengers from the Lusitania has been landed here from boats. Ten or eleven boatloads came ashore, and others are expected."

The motor boat Elizabeth has arrived at Kinsale and reports that at 3:30 p. m. she picked up two lifeboats containing 63 and 16 survivors of the Lusitania, respectively. A Cork tug took the rescued to Queenstown. They were mostly women and children.

The Lusitania could not launch many of her lifeboats.

The tiny hospitals of Kinsale and Clonakilty, and the institutions at Cork and Queenstown are jammed with survivors from the ocean horror, those not actually wounded suffering terribly from shock. The giant Cunarder now rests on the bottom of the ocean about eight miles off Kinsale Head and twenty miles from the entrance to Queenstown Harbor.

ADMIRALTY GIVES OUT NEWS.

Telegrams have been filtering into London last night and early this morning stating that the rescued are being brought to Queenstown by three steamers. The Admiralty says between 600 and six hundred have already been landed at Clonakilty and Kinsale, coming into the latter port in a string of boats towed by a Greek steamer. Motor fishing boats hovered near the scene of the wreck, picking up what boats they could and turning them over to the powerful ocean going tug Stormcock.

Huge crowds fill Cockspur Street near the Haymarket, storming the Cunard offices for news. The women, who had been weeping so bitterly, paused for a moment when an agent of the line bellowed through a megaphone the following dispatch:

"Our Liverpool office says First Officer Jones wires from Queenstown he thinks between five hundred and six hundred have been saved. This includes passengers and crew, and is only an estimate."

A steward in the first boat which landed at Kinsale said feared that 900 lives had been lost.

THE LUSITANIA, SUNK BY GERMAN TORPEDO, WITH HEAVY LOSS OF LIFE.

FIRST SURVIVORS' NAMES RECEIVED

The first names of survivors of the Lusitania disaster received here are as follows:

Lassetter, General, and son, first cabin, Boorhamton, Mrs. second cabin.
Smith, George A., New York, wine merchant.
Smith, Mrs. J. T., Braceville, Ohio.

SOUTH COAST OF IRELAND

Showing—here the Lusitania was attacked and the points where survivors of the passengers and crew were landed.

Chapter 2

The War Clouds Gather

It is often thought that it was the sinking of the 32,000-ton ocean liner *Lusitania* off the coast of Ireland by the German submarine *U-20* on 7 May 1915 that brought the United States of America into the First World War. The incident arose when the commander of *U-20*, *Kapitänleutnant* Walter Schwieger, had seen a ship some fourteen miles' distant and identified her, according to his 1914 copy of *Jane's Fighting Ships* and the *Naval Annual*, as an armed merchant cruiser believed by Germany to be used as a troopship. In his boat's log, Schwieger wrote:

2:20 p.m. Directly in front of us I sighted four funnels and masts of a

RMS Lusitania.

Kapitänleutnant *Walter Schwieger – captain of the* U-20.

steamer at right angles to our course, coming from south-south-west and going toward Galley Head. It is recognised as a passenger steamer.

2:25 p.m. Have advanced eleven metres toward steamer, in hope it will change course along the Irish coast.

2:35 p.m. Steamer turns, takes direction to Queenstown, and thereby makes it possible for us to approach it for shot. We proceed at high speed in order to reach correct position.

3:10 p.m. Torpedo shot at distance of 700 metres, going 3 metres below the surface. Hits steering centre behind bridge. Unusually great detonation with large cloud of smoke and debris shot above the funnels. In addition to torpedo, a second explosion must have taken place. (Boiler, coal or powder?) Bridge and part of the ship where the torpedo hit are torn apart and

The German submarine U-20 *that sank the RMS* Lusitania.

fire follows. The ship stops and very quickly leans over to starboard, at the same time sinking at the bow. It looks as though it would capsize in a short time. There is great confusion on board. Boats are cleared and many of them lowered into the water. Many boats, fully loaded, drop down into the water bow- or stern-first and capsize. The boats on the port side cannot be made clear because of the slanting position. At the front of the ship the name *Lusitania* in gold letters can be seen. The chimneys are painted black. The stern flag is not hoisted. The ship was going about twenty miles an hour.

Twenty minutes later the liner plunged to the bottom of the Atlantic, leaving 1,198 passengers and crewmen, among them 35 children and 135 Americans (one of whom was the multi-millionaire Alfred G. Vanderbilt), to die in its cold waters. There were just 761 survivors of this horrendous attack. Schwieger maintained that he never realised the ship was the *Lusitania* until, on looking through his periscope, he saw the ship's name in gold letters on the bows as she was sinking. On his return to Wilhelmshaven, Germany, Schwieger was warmly congratulated by other members of the submarine fraternity, but received a severe reprimand from the Kaiser for having sunk the liner. This angered many of the submarine commanders as they maintained that Schwieger was just following the orders issued by the Kaiser's military advisers, *and* with his full knowledge.

On 1 May, the day the *Lusitania* left New York on her fateful voyage, an American oil tanker, the *Gulflight*, was struck by a torpedo from the German submarine *U-30*, off the Scilly Isles. Three of the tanker's crew were killed in the incident. The captain died of a heart attack and the other two crew members died when they jumped overboard, and

RMS Lusitania *leaving New York on her fateful voyage.*

The American oil tanker Gulflight *showing the gaping hole caused by a torpedo.*

although the ship was severely damaged, it managed to limp back to port under its own steam. The Germans claimed it was a case of mistaken identity and apologised profusely, but *The New York Times* bannered the incident as a 'flagrant violation of our rights'.

These violations were further aggravated by the sinking of the 15,000-ton White Star transatlantic passenger liner *Arabic,* again off the coast of southern Ireland, on 19 August 1915, by the German submarine *U-24* under the command of *Kapitänleutnant* Schneider. The liner, with its 429 passengers and crew aboard, was en route to New York when it was torpedoed. Forty-four passengers died in the incident, three of them Americans, when the liner sank in less than ten minutes after being struck by the torpedo. The German explana-

tion, which the Americans totally rejected, was that the submarine was in the process of a perfectly 'legitimate' act of war – sinking the British merchant ship *Dunsley,* by shell-fire – when the *Arabic* appeared on the scene. According to the German U-boat commander Schneider, the liner appeared to change her course and he was convinced that his submarine was about to be rammed and had fired a torpedo at the *Arabic* in self-defence.

This incident was followed shortly afterwards by the sinking of the 10,920-ton liner *Hesperian* off Fastnet on 6 September 1915 by the submarine *U-20,* with the loss of 32 lives. *U-20,* commanded by *Kapitänleutnant* Schwieger, who earlier that year had sunk the *Lusitania,* again pleaded mistaken identity. And no sooner had the crisis over this and the other

The liner Arabic.

atrocities been averted than news came through about the sinking of the Italian liner *Ancona* by an Austro-Hungarian submarine. The Austro-Hungarian Empire was allied to Germany at the time, and the incident was particularly brutal inasmuch as the liner was fired upon and sunk while the passengers were in the process of trying to escape into the lifeboats.

Another incident concerned the Royal Navy. It came about through an attack on 18 August 1915 by the German submarine *U-27*, commanded by *Kapitänleutnant* Bernhardt Wegener, on a British–Irish crewed cargo ship,

The mule ship SS Nicosian.

The Q-ship Baralong.

One of the concealed guns aboard the Q-ship Baralong.

The German submarine U-41 *photographed from the cargo ship* Urbino *before the appearance of the Q-ship* Baralong.

the 6,359-ton *Nicosian,* that was carrying 780 mules and eighty American muleteers to Britain. The crew and muleteers had taken to the lifeboats after their ship had been stopped by *U-27* and were watching the submarine attempt to sink their vessel when a Royal Navy Q-ship (armed decoy ship used as an anti-submarine weapon), the *Baralong,* arrived and sank the submarine with gunfire. Eleven members of the U-boat's crew who survived the shelling swam towards the now abandoned cargo ship. Six of them were shot by the crew of the Q-ship as they tried to get aboard; the

remaining five, who had managed to clamber aboard the ship, were later shot by British marines after they had boarded the vessel. The damage to the *Nicosian* was slight, and after a makeshift crew had been put back aboard a tow line was rigged between the two ships and the long haul to Avonmouth Docks, Bristol, began. They were joined later by the armed yacht HMS *Valiant,* which continued to escort both ships into port.

The incident, which was related to the US authorities some months later by the muleteers, caused an outcry from the German

Shot taken from the SS Urbino, *showing the* U-41 *blowing up after being shelled by the Q-ship* Baralong.

authorities and the pro-German press in the United States over the 'barbarity' of the British Royal Navy. The fact that the *Baralong* had saved the lives of the muleteers and the crew of the *Nicosian* seemed to have eluded them. This incident was further aggravated one month later when the *Baralong* sank *U-41* with only two survivors. These two crewmen complained bitterly about the harsh treatment they said they had received at the hands of the Royal Navy. *U-41* was in the process of trying to sink the unarmed cargo ship SS *Urbino* when the *Baralong* arrived on the scene. Much public feeling at this stage appeared to have forgotten about the war being waged by German submarines on unarmed liners and their civilian passengers, many of which were Americans.

Although these terrible acts of aggression on unarmed ocean-going vessels had a significant impact upon America's relationship with Germany, it was an accumulation of these and a number of other incidents that were to be instrumental in bringing the United States of America into the war. The final act of treachery and deception, however, was the interception of the now infamous Zimmermann telegram. This telegram, from Arthur Zimmermann, Germany's Foreign Minister, to the German Ambassador von Eckhardt in Mexico, had been intercepted by British Naval Intelligence. The head of British Naval Intelligence at the time was Admiral Sir Reginald Hall, who, together with his small team of cryptologists, decoded the message and handed it over to the American Ambassador in London, Walter Page. At the same time the British team also handed over the 'key' to unlocking Germany's cryptic messages, thus enabling the United States' intelligence organisation to decode any German messages intercepted by them. It was said later that the decoding of the message was to have consequences that no one at the time could ever have envisaged. The message read:

Berlin. Jan.19.1917.

On the 1st February we intend to begin submarine warfare unrestricted. In spite of this, it is our intention to endeavour to keep neutral the United States of America.

If this attempt is not successful, we propose an alliance on the following basis with Mexico: That we shall make war together and together make peace. We shall give general financial support, and it is understood that Mexico is to reconquer the lost territory of New Mexico, Texas and Arizona. The details are left to you for settlement.

You are instructed to inform the President of Mexico of the above in the greatest confidence as soon as it is certain that there will be an outbreak of war with the United States, and suggest that the President of Mexico, on his own initiative, should communicate with Japan suggesting adherence at once to this plan. At the same time, offer to mediate between Germany and Japan.

Please call to the attention of the President of Mexico that the employment of ruthless submarine warfare now promises to compel England to make peace in a few months.

Zimmermann

The decoded message was immediately flashed to President Wilson, and, despite the strenuous denials of the German government, it essentially ended the uneasy peace that had

Captain Reginald Hall – Director of British Naval Intelligence.

existed between America and Germany.

On 3 February 1917 President Woodrow Wilson announced to the American Congress that all diplomatic relations with the German Empire had been severed. Even at this stage there was still uncertainty as to whether or not the United States would actually go to war, but on 18 March 1917 news came that was to inflame the American people even more. It was announced from London that three American steamships – the *City of Memphis*, the *Illinois* and *Vigilancia* – had been sunk by a German submarine. The *City of Memphis* and *Vigilancia* were sunk without warning, resulting in a total loss of life of those on board; the exception was the oil tanker *Illinois*, which was steaming through the English Channel on 18 March 1917, on its way home to Texas. It had a large pair of American flags and the initials U.S.A. painted on its sides. A German submarine

President Woodrow Wilson addressing Congress on 2 April 1917.

The American oil tanker Illinois *sinking after being torpedoed by a German U-boat on 18 March 1917.*

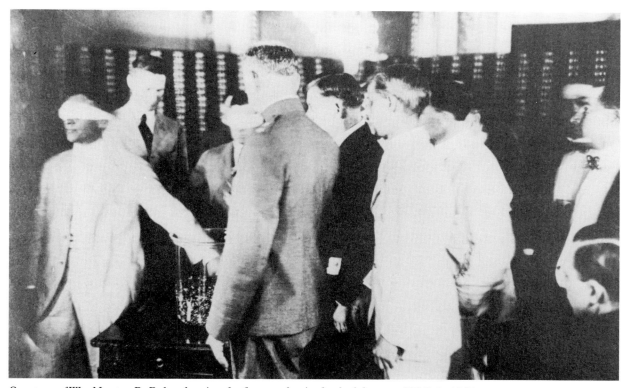

Secretary of War Newton D. Baker drawing the first number in the draft lottery of 20 July 1917.

stopped the tanker, boarded, plundered, then destroyed it by setting off bombs in the oil compartments. The fate of the crew remains a mystery, but it is unlikely that the submarine commander would have killed them in cold blood, more likely they were left to their own fate in their lifeboats – which in the minds of many is tantamount to the same thing.

Two months later, on 2 April 1917, President Wilson asked Congress to declare that a state of war existed between the United States and Germany. By 6 April both houses had passed the resolution and the United States officially declared war. A total of 25,000 men of the National Guard, along with some 2,000 sailors, were ordered to stand by and ready themselves for war. Congress then debated whether or not to introduce a draft system, but as one opponent, Champ Clark, the Speaker of the House of Congress,

announced, 'In the estimation of Missourians, there is precious little difference between a conscript and a convict.' However, an act was passed ordering that men in their twenties must register for the draft of 5 June, and on that day 9,660,000 men registered. On the morning of 20 July, Secretary of War Newton D. Baker reached into a large glass jar containing 10,500 numbers, the largest number in any registration district, and took out a capsule bearing the number 258. The man holding that number in each district throughout the United States was the first to be called to arms.

Funds were made available to the President, and America was about to embark on the biggest test of its resources and manpower since the War of Independence, only this time Britain was to be its ally. By the time the war ended, America would have contributed in excess of $35,000,000,000 to the Allied effort,

German Ambassador to the United States Count Bernstorff.

America. There was also a faction in America that encouraged the war, not out of any form of patriotism or hatred of the Germans, but because they were munitions and military hardware manufacturers and could see a path to enormous profits.

The American Ambassador in Berlin, Mr James W. Gerard, was recalled at the beginning of February, and the German Ambassador to the United States, Count Johann von Bernstorff, had his passport returned and was asked to leave the country. The German government reacted immediately by cutting the telephone wires to the American Embassy in Berlin, interfering with all the mail, withholding the ambassador's passport and removing all his diplomatic privileges – 'holding the ambassador hostage,' as they put it, 'for the proper treatment of their ambassador, Count Bernstorff, and the crews of the German ships in the United States'. The Americans replied that all official German property would be 'immune from seizure and their persons from molestation so long as they behaved

75,280 of her men would have been killed in action, 201,847 wounded and 8,668 would be prisoners-of-war or missing. And all in a matter of just 18 months. The cost in resources was enormous, but the cost in human lives and suffering was incalculable.

It was also a time of anguish and heart-searching for the American people, mainly because of their multinational population, which of course included a large number of Germans. It was discovered later that a number of German Americans had returned to Germany to fight against Britain and France – and, ultimately, their adopted country,

James W. Gerard, US Ambassador to Germany – 1913–1917.

An American war bond poster depicting the sinking of the hospital ship Llandovery Castle.

The German submarine U-86, *commanded by* Oberleutnant *Helmut Patzig, which sank the hospital ship* Llandovery Castle.

themselves'. Encouraged by this, and the fact that they realised they were only aggravating the situation, the Germans released Gerard and his staff, who immediately returned to the United States.

The Germans, now faced with an even greater adversary, went after nearly all the shipping in the Atlantic, and among these a number of unarmed merchant ships, including the British hospital ship *Llandovery Castle*, which was sunk by the submarine *U-86*. On the night of 27 June 1918, the clearly marked hospital ship had been sighted by the German submarine 116 miles off Fastnet Rock, off the coast of southern Ireland. The ship was torpedoed and the ship's crew took to the lifeboats. Fortunately there were no wounded aboard, but there were 14 nurses. After surfacing, the commander of the submarine, *Oberleutnant* Helmut Patzig, spoke to the captain of the

Llandovery Castle, Captain R.A. Sylvester, demanding to know about the 8 American airmen that were on board. It was pointed out by Captain Sylvester that there were seven Canadian medical officers aboard and that was probably where the confusion lay (it was never discovered how the Germans knew who was on board). *Oberleutnant* Patzig, according to Captain Sylvester, turned away in anger, fired upon the survivors and then ran down the remaining lifeboats, smashing them like matchwood and spilling those left alive into the water. In all 234 hospital staff, including the 14 nurses and 34 crew members, died at the hands of Patzig and his crew. The only survivors were those in the captain's lifeboat. This unparalleled act of inhumanity caused outrage around the world, and there were violent anti-German demonstrations in Britain, America, Australia and South Africa.

Chapter 3

May 1916 – December 1917:
War Becomes a Reality

Congress, in 1916, had made available some funds for the development of the National Guard Aviation Units, a number of which were already in service using privately owned aircraft. The first to take advantage of the funds was New York State, and within a matter of months the 1st Aero Company, NYNG (New York National Guard), based at Mineola, was formed, with twenty-six officers and twelve enlisted ranks. With additional funding from the Aero Club of America, Mineola soon became the recognised airfield to which students from the Curtiss School at Newport News, Virginia, and the Thomas School at Ithaca, New York, were sent to be qualified as Reserve Military Aviators. Because of the increased need for facilities to train these new aviators, the Governor's Island Aviation School in New York was moved to Mineola to be amalgamated with the 1st Aero Company.

The beginning of May 1916 saw the appearance of the *Escadrille Lafayette*. The squadron was named after the Marquis de Lafayette who had helped the American colonials in their fight for independence against King George III of England in 1777. The *Escadrille Lafayette* was a French–American squadron comprising American volunteer pilots and regular French military pilots. It was to leave its mark in the

First World War, helping to lay the foundations of an air force that was to become a world leader in later years.

The squadron had started when young American adventurers decided to go and fight in the war in Europe. Some joined the RFC (Royal Flying Corps) while others joined the Foreign Legion. After training as pilots, they joined with French pilots in the *Service Aéronautique*. Initially there was a certain reluctance on the part of the French to accept American volunteer airmen. This had come about because earlier in the war a German airman had joined the *Service Aéronautique* by means of a forged American passport. He caused considerable damage by feeding back intelligence on French air activities and aircraft, before being discovered and shot as a spy. In July 1915, Dr Edmund Gros and Jarousse de Sillac hosted a luncheon party at the home of a friend, Senator Gaston Ménièr. The list of guests included Colonel Bouttieaux, Leon Bourgeois and a guest of honour, General Auguste Hirshauer, the head of French military aeronautics. Before the day was over, General Hirshauer had agreed in principle to the formation of an all-American squadron. But with more and more Americans arriving in France to join in the war, it was decided to form an all-American squadron,

Escadrille Lafayette *pilots at Chaudun in July 1917. L-R Front Row: Masson, Bigelow, Johnson, Thaw, Thenault, Parsons, Hewitt, Willis, Havilland. L-R Rear: Bridgeman, Rockwell, Jones, Peterson, Dugan, MacMonagle, Lovell, de Maison-Rouge.*

L'Escadrille Américaine. But after protests by the German Ambassador in France and other pro-German groups in the United States, who said it was the *Escadrille des Volontaires* and in violation of the Hague convention (Article 6, Chapter 1, Convention V), the name was changed to the Lafayette Flying Corps, although its official name was *Escadrille de Chasse Nieuport (N) 124.*

Among the founders of this soon-to-become-famous squadron were Captain Georges Thenault and Lieutenants Arnoux de Laage de Mieux, Victor Chapman, Norman Prince, James McConnell, Kiffen Rockwell, William Thaw, Elliott Cowdin, Clyde Balsley, Charles Johnson, Bert Hall and Lawrence

Rumsey. In later years over four thousand men would lay claim to having flown with the *Escadrille Lafayette*, but in reality only thirty-eight Americans and four French officers ever officially numbered among its flying personnel. (A complete list of all members can be found in Appendix 2.) What set these men apart was the fact that they were nearly all college-educated, from well-to-do families. They could have spent the rest of their lives in comfort, but chose to fight either out of a love of adventure or out of a sense of idealism. Some, however, came from different backgrounds, such as Bert Hall. Hall was *the* 'American in Paris', a Paris taxi driver who became disillusioned with the scope of his job and joined the Legion.

Lt Andrew Campbell of the Escadrille Lafayette *with a relieved smile on his face, standing in the gap where his portside lower wing used to be.*

The idea of an all-American squadron of volunteers, it is said, was first proposed by William Thaw. Thaw had learned to fly at the Curtiss Flying School at Hammondsport, New York in 1913 and soon made himself a reputation as a pilot who could take chances and survive. His background was that of a young man who came from an extremely wealthy family and enjoyed all the comforts that money could buy. His father was a director of a number of large companies, including the Pennsylvania Railroad, and allowed his son virtually unlimited funds. It was while on a visit to the Riviera that war broke out, and Thaw immediately offered his services as an aviator to the French government. They turned him down on the grounds that they had more volunteers to fly aircraft than they had aircraft. They also did not want any foreigners in their army at that point of the war.

Thaw would not take no for an answer, and together with forty-two other Americans went to the Hôtel des Invalides on 21 August 1914 and enlisted in the Foreign Legion as a common *soldat*. He convinced the French authorities that he had served with the American forces in Mexico and explained his lack of drill experience by saying that he had been part of a guerrilla outfit. He was enrolled into the Second Regiment of the Foreign Legion and was sent to the Champagne sector, and, it was while at the Front, holding a section of the line

Major William K. Thaw and Lt-Col Ralph Royce.

Thaw was not the only American who had had ideas about an all-American squadron. Norman Prince, a graduate lawyer from Harvard University, who, like Thaw, had learned to fly in 1913, offered his services to the French government and was accepted. Thaw, when his second attempt to join the French Aviation Service was successful, met up with Norman Prince and Bert Hall. One thing led to another and the French authorities decided to include the American volunteers in one of their squadrons for training. After a great deal of training, the original members won their brevets, then other American volunteers arrived. After some discussion among representatives of both the American and French governments and the promise of financial support from a group of wealthy American businessmen, Squadron N. 124 was formed.

The distinctive head of a Seminole Indian chief, later replaced with the head of a Sioux Indian chief, was painted on the fuselage of the SPAD (*Société Pour Aviation et ses Dérivés*) VII.CI aircraft and became the insignia of the legendary *Escadrille Lafayette*. The squadron was supported and financed by many wealthy and influential Americans who believed that the United States should be actively engaged in the war as an ally of Britain and France; for some, of course, there was an alternative and ulterior motive: they saw ways and means of turning the war into a profitable enterprise by manufacturing war materials. Initially called the Franco-American Committee, the name was later changed to the Lafayette Flying Corps Committee with William K. Vanderbilt as honorary president, Jarousse de Sillac as president and Dr Edmund Gros as vice-president, and it was they who conceived the idea of financing an American fighting unit in the French Air Service. The idea was to have American heroes in French uniforms, fighting for freedom in this new and colourful element of warfare. This, it was hoped, would lend publicity to the raising of funds in America to support the cause. This was a very Hollywood-sounding description, and one that was to

at Verzeney, that he came up with the idea of an all-American squadron of fighter aircraft after a squadron of German fighters had flown overhead. He voiced his ideas to the other American pilots he knew, but that was as far as it got for the time being. One American who was trying to enlist, actually went as far as persuading the French to recruit him into the Legion, after telling them that he had served for five years in the Salvation Army.

The SPAD S.XIII of Lt Robert Soubrian when with the Escadrille Lafayette. *Excellent shot of the Seminole Chief insignia on the fuselage.*

Four American members of the Escadrille Lafayette, *all of whom died within a few months of the photograph being taken. L-R: James McConnell, Kiffin Rockwell, Georges Thenault, Norman Prince and Victor Chapman.*

rapidly disillusion those who later fought in the war.

There was a considerable amount of opposition to involvement in the war from many groups, especially those that had members whose ancestry was German. A great deal of pressure was put upon the government to try and dissuade them from entering the war, and for a while the government resisted the urge. But then, during the following year, the maritime incidents described in chapter 2 occurred, forcing the United States to take action and join her long-time ally Great Britain in the fight against Germany.

When America declared war on Germany, there were only five United States aviation officers in Europe: three were at French flying schools undergoing instruction, one was the assistant military attaché in London, and the remaining one was Major William 'Billy' Mitchell, who was acting as an observer in Spain. With the onset of the war, Mitchell immediately made his way to Britain entirely on his own initiative and set up a meeting with Major-General Trenchard, who was commander of the Independent Air Force at that time. With the help of Trenchard, Mitchell constructed a plan that he could present to General Pershing. The plan consisted of two types of air force: one in effect a development of pursuit squadrons, the other of bomber squadrons. It was because of General Trenchard's contribution and influence that the plan, in principle, was accepted and a board of officers convened to create the Air Service, AEF (American Expeditionary Force).

The board, however, was more inclined to create an independent strategic Air Force than an air force that was controlled by the army. General Pershing realised this, but saw the Air Force as part of the Army under his control. He dismissed the idea proposed by the board, who had been guided and were very impressed by the British and French strategic bombing squadrons, and insisted that units were trained for missions in support of and in participation with the Army. Although there were moves to try and give the Air Force some independence, aside from the odd occasional pursuit and bombardment missions they stayed under the auspices of the Army throughout the war. In fact it was not until September 1947, after the end of the Second World War, that the Army relinquished its hold over the Air Force.

The war, however one looked at it, was a war for artillery and infantry, and balloons and aircraft were, according to the sceptics, only there for support. The heavy artillery, in these early years, caused more devastation than the bomber aircraft ever did, but it was the reconnaissance flights and spotting missions carried out by the aviation section that were primarily responsible for the success of the artillery. By the end of the war the aviation section had proved its worth beyond all doubt and had been grudgingly accepted by the sceptics as 'having done their bit'.

The United States Navy, meanwhile, had not restricted their direction and movements solely towards the sea. On the declaration of war against Germany, naval aviation strength stood at 48 officers and 239 enlisted men, all with aviation experience of one kind or another. They had 54 aircraft, all training types, 1 free balloon, 1 kite balloon, 1 very suspect dirigible and 1 air station. The navy had started training pilots and crews some 6 years earlier, but had fallen into a limbo period over the last year, mainly because of the number of accidents they had had. In the main, this was not the fault of the instructors or students, but of the aircraft themselves. It has to be remembered that the aircraft industry in America, as in Europe, was still in the learning stages of development and some of the aircraft coming out of the factories left a lot to be desired. The main source of American aircraft was Britain and France.

Over $3 million had been set aside by Congress for the US Navy's Naval Flying Corps, as it was known in the Naval Appropriation Act of 29 August 1916; unfortunately, none of the funding appeared to find

The cruiser USS Huntington *with its kite balloon aloft. A Curtiss N-9H seaplane can be seen aboard, whilst another seaplane can be seen flying in the distance on the far right.*

its way into the Navy's coffers. The Naval Flying Corps had not been officially established, and although suitable sites for air bases had been selected along the east coast, all were in the planning stages. Late in 1916 the first of the Curtiss N-9s were delivered to the Navy and experiments were started with shipboard catapults aboard the USS *North Carolina*, the USS *Huntington* and the USS *Seattle*. In Britain, France, Germany, Italy and the Austro-Hungarian Empire, naval aviation was being actively encouraged, leaving the United States woefully behind. But interest was growing and a number of wealthy young men at the various universities in America

decided to buy their own aircraft and hire instructors to teach them.

Among these was F. Trubee Davison of Yale University, who formed the First Yale Unit, which was later incorporated into Aerial Coastal Patrol Unit (CPU) No. 1. This CPU was the brainchild of Rear-Admiral Robert E. Peary and Henry Woodhouse, both ardent believers in naval aviation who raised money from individual contributions to form the National Coastal Patrol Commission. This encouraged Curtiss and other enterprising manufacturers to set up flying training schools, not only for pilots, but for mechanics and engineers to keep the aircraft flying. Although

Davison had a number of students at Yale ready to learn to fly, he still had the problem of finding enough aircraft and instructors to meet their needs. Just outside New York on Long Island, a Philadelphia merchant by the name of Rodman Wanamaker operated a flying school at Port Washington. After lengthy consultations with him, Davison managed to persuade him to let them use his Curtiss flying boat and one instructor by the name of David McCulloch. McCulloch was later to join the Navy and gain fame as the co-pilot of the NC-3 flying boat on the US Navy's successful attempt to become the first to fly the Atlantic Ocean. Only one of the four NC aircraft, the NC-4, made it.

The summer of 1917 saw the first twelve members of the First Yale Unit at Locust Valley clambering all over the Curtiss flying boat, maintaining it, cleaning it and learning to fly.

1st Lt Trubee Davison, USN prior to his flying training.

1st Lt Alfred Cunningham, USMC.

Aerial Coastal Patrol Unit No. 1.

By the end of the summer four of the students had flown solo and the remaining eight were ready. Towards the end of the year, the students were invited to take part as members of the Aerial Coastal Patrol in the manoeuvres off Sandy Hook with battleships, destroyers and coastal boats. So successful were the manoeuvres, and so impressed with the standard of flying were the military and civilians, that the faculty was given two more seaplanes and additional funding. In March 1917 the whole unit was transferred to West Palm Beach, Florida, to take advantage of the weather and to finalise the remaining elements of their flying training. All members of the First Yale Unit were enrolled into the US Navy and a naval

lieutenant was placed in command. One month later the unit returned to Long Island and began the business of flight training in readiness for war.

The US Marine Corps had not been idle either, and aviation essentially started for them on 22 May 1912 when the first marine aviator, 1st Lieutenant A.A. Cunningham, reported for his initial flight training at Annapolis, Maryland. After receiving his ground instruction, Cunningham was posted to the Burgess Aircraft Factory for flight training itself, and on 1 August 1912, after two hours of training, he soloed and was designated Naval Aviator No. 5. Two more marines followed that year, Lieutenant Bernard L. Smith and 2nd

Captain Roy Geiger, USMC.

Lieutenant William M. McLivain. But it was not until June 1915 when the next marine, 1st Lieutenant Francis T. Evans, reported for training, followed on 31 March 1916 by 1st Lieutenant Roy Geiger, that the nucleus of USMC Aviation was formed.

On 7 April 1917, the day after the United States had declared war on Germany, the President directed that control of the US Coast Guard be transferred from the Treasury department to the US Navy. The same month also saw the formation of the Marine Aeronautical Company, Advance Base Force at the marine barracks in the Philadelphia Navy Yard, under the command of Captain A.A. Cunningham. The company was made up from the Marine Aviation Section at US Aeronautical Station, Pensacola, Florida, and the Marine Corps Reserve Flying Corps, and comprised 34 officers and 330 enlisted men with 2 Curtiss R-6 seaplanes and 1 Farman

land version.

The Marine Aeronautical Company was divided into two units, the First Marine Aeronautic Company and the First Aviation Squadron, commanded by Captain Francis T. Evans and comprising 10 officers and 93 enlisted men. The First Marine Aeronautic Company moved to the Navy Coastal Air Station at Cape May, New Jersey, on 14 October 1917 for seaplane and coastal patrol training. The First Aviation Squadron, commanded by Captain McLivain, comprised 24 officers and 237 enlisted men and started flight training at the Army Aviation School at Hazelhurst Field, Mineola, Long Island, New York, the same month. Because of the increasingly inclement weather, the 1st Aviation Squadron, as it became known, moved south to the US Army's Gerstner Field at Lake Charles, Louisiana.

After extensive training, the First Marine Aeronautic Squadron, complete with its complement of 10 Curtiss R-6 seaplanes, 2 N-9 seaplanes and 6 Curtiss HS-1 flying boats, 12 officers and 133 enlisted men, boarded the USS *Hancock* in the Philadelphia Navy Yard. Their destination was Ponta Delada in the Azores, where throughout the war they maintained a constant daylight patrol of the Western Approaches. They were the first fully trained and equipped flying unit from the United States to operate overseas. The squadron carried out patrols around the waters that surrounded the islands from dawn to dusk, and the only sighting they had of the enemy was on 11 September 1918. A Curtiss R-6 was on patrol with pilot Lt Walter Poague and his crew member, Gunnery Sergeant Zeigler, when they sighted a German U-boat on the surface. They circled, then came in to attack and drop their one and only bomb. Unfortunately not only did the bomb miss, it also failed to explode, and the two flyers could only watch as the submarine's crew leisurely battened down the hatches and then submerged out of sight.

A further unit from within the First Aviation Force was formed, under the command of

Captain Roy Geiger, USMC. This unit, comprising four officers and thirty-six enlisted men, was ordered to Miami, Florida, where they took over a small airfield owned by the Curtiss Flying School. After extensive training and the influx of a number of fully trained pilots from the US Navy, the First Marine Aviation Force was mobilised for France and its first taste of war.

The first flight of the Navy's first airship, a B Class model, was successful after making the trip from Chicago, Illinois, where it was made, to Akron, Ohio. It was flown by a Goodyear pilot by the name of R.H. Upson. A second flight in the airship, designated DN-1 by the Navy and flown by Lt-Cdr Frank R. McCrary, USN, was made from Pensacola, but was a dismal failure. Even after extensive modifications and testing the results were the same, and only two more flights followed before the airship was finally grounded for the last time. But the Lighter-Than-Air programme supported by the Goodyear Tire and Rubber Company was

slowly gaining momentum. Goodyear had agreed with the Navy that they would provide the facilities and the equipment; all the Navy had to do was provide the trainees. The school opened on a field located at Fritsche's Lake (later called Wingfoot), three miles from the town of Akron. It consisted of a hangar 400 × 100 × 100 feet, tool and equipment shops, classrooms, barracks for the students and quarters for the officers. Within six months the first eight men had qualified and were designated Naval Aviators (Dirigibles), but it was to be a further two months before they were assigned to their units.

Later, another training base was set up at Pensacola, Florida. Contracts to five different companies had been awarded for sixteen new B Class airships, all based on a similar design and to the specifications laid down by the Navy. As crews became more competent, coastal patrols from naval air stations were commenced. The airships operated from NAS Chatham, Massachusetts; Cape May, New

NAS Pensacola with three Curtiss H-12s on the slipway.

Jersey; Rockaway Beach and Montauk Point, New York; and Key West, Florida. Although the airships that carried out these coastal patrols proved to be extremely useful weapons, not one was ever used in Europe. Trained LTA (Lighter Than Air) pilots were sent to NAS Paimboeuf in France, where they carried out familiarisation training in French airships before going on active service patrols.

The use of manned kite balloons on battleships and destroyers for observation purposes was a direct spin-off from the airships. These balloons, unlike the airships, were tethered to the ships and had no directional movement other than up and down, save that of the ship's own movement. Their purpose was to spot for enemy warships or submarines, but this was controlled by the weather. If the seas were relatively calm, then the observation kite balloon was launched, but if there were high seas running or it was foggy, then it was impracticable.

Experiments were also started with a guided-missile programme after funding of $50,000 had been allocated by the Secretary of the Navy. The work centred around the use of aerial torpedoes in the form of automatic, gyroscopically controlled aircraft. The results were at first encouraging, but the longer they went on the more expensive they got and the project was shelved. It was resurrected during the Second World War, but only used on a couple of occasions.

The first national insignia designed for United States aircraft was ordered to be placed on all naval aircraft. It was a red disc within a white star on a blue circular field on the wings, and red, white and blue vertical stripes with blue forward on the rudder. One of the main reasons for the insignia was the increasing number of incidents in which US aircraft were fired upon by their own troops, and it was deemed to be necessary to educate the ground troops in the simplest way.

In June 1917, Brigadier-General William L. Kenly, a field artillery officer, arrived in Paris to set up the Air Service headquarters of the American Expeditionary Force (AEF) and

take up the post of Chief of Air Service. He was accompanied by Colonel Raynal C. Bolling, Assistant Chief in Charge of Supply, and Colonel William Mitchell, Air Commander, Zone of Advance. They had plenty of ideas, but no aircraft. The relative calm was short-lived when, on 27 November, Brigadier-General B.D. Foulis arrived in France complete with a ready-made headquarters staff comprising 112 officers and 300 men. Within two days he had replaced Brigadier-General Kenly as Chief of Air Staff and moved his own team into the headquarters. The resentment created by the sudden move also caused organisational problems, one side refusing to co-operate with the other. There were also other obstacles, brought about in the main by jealousies and friction between the aviation and ground staffs. Major Frederick

Major (later Colonel) Raynal C. Bolling, USAS.

Palmer, a senior member of Brigadier-General Foulis's staff, wrote in a letter to a friend:

> Every whim of these flyers was unwritten law to the ground forces on the flying field, who [were] expected to have M'Lord's steed ready for him to mount before he rode forth to the tournament of the skies; and his bath drawn in his pleasant quarters, ready for him on his return. Some of the glamour was rapidly disappearing, as it was discovered that the ability to fly was not uncommon and there were no end of volunteers for aviation. The same could not be said for the common soldier. Aces had their communiqués, whilst the surviving officer of a veteran battalion which took its objectives amidst suffering horrendous losses, was not mentioned. Ascending, well-groomed and well-fed, to death in a plane seemed quite pleasant when compared to going over top from filthy trenches, to be mashed up in No Mans Land among putrid corpses.

Back in the United States, Congress had allocated a staggering $640 million to the air programme and then set about convincing the general public and the media that it was justified. This at first angered General Pershing, who thought the extra money spent on convincing the public would be better spent on establishing the Air Service. But he had problems of his own within the structure of his senior officers, and although his contemptuous attitude towards the new Air Service had not changed one iota, he had the foresight to realise the potential of such a service. Pershing was convinced that the war would be won on the ground, and the Air Arm's role would just be as a support to the infantry and artillery. The problem with his senior officers was resolved on 29 May 1918 when he replaced the Chief of the Air Service, Brigadier-General

Kenly, with one of his own men, Brigadier-General Mason M. Patrick, an old class-mate. Pershing also recommended that increased pay and rank for men engaged in flying duties be abolished.

General Pershing's view of the usefulness of the Air Service was guided by the number of experienced aviation specialists under his command, which amounted to very few. One of these was Major Frank P. Lahm, who was an expert on military balloons. He had received his balloonist's certificate in 1905 and his pilot's rating in 1909. In May 1917, Lahm had been given command of the Army's balloon school at Fort Omaha, Nebraska, but in August was sent to France to study French and British balloon training and their operations under battlefield conditions. He was ordered to return to the United States in the December, but General Pershing intervened saying that Lahm's expertise was required by the AEF.

The need for balloon companies at the Front increased. There were only four balloon companies in France at the time supporting the infantry: the 1st, 2nd, 3rd and 4th, who made up the 2nd Balloon Squadron. Training was of the essence, and training under battlefield conditions even more so. In the United States military balloon training was virtually non-existent compared to Europe, even though there had been a balloon section in the US Army Signal Corps in existence since 1891. A number of officers had been sent to Europe at the time to study at the French *Aérostation*, but unfortunately all the information acquired was soon forgotten, so in 1917 an advanced school was set up at Cuperly-sur-Marne, France, close to the French balloon school at Vadenay. This school did not last long because during the German offensive of March 1918 it came under intense, heavy attack, so it was decided to move it to Souge, between the Gironde and Dordogne rivers in south-west France, close to the city of Bordeaux.

Students at the school soon discovered that

A US Signal Corps balloon windlass with caterpillar tracks.

A German anti-aircraft battery in action against a US observation balloon.

A US Signal Corps observation balloon being winched up by its winch truck.

being a member of a balloon company was not a soft option. Because of the nature of their role of information-gatherers, the balloons were close to the Front and rapidly became targets for enemy artillery, small-arms fire and attacks by aircraft. Not only were the observers in the balloons' baskets at risk, so were the ground crews. The balloon had to be filled with 23,000 cubic feet of inflammable hydrogen, so around the balloon area there was not only a winch truck, but trucks carrying large numbers of gas cylinders. Because they were regarded as a very serious threat by both sides, balloon companies became important targets and were

subjected to heavy shelling with high-explosive shells. As can easily be imagined, the results of a direct hit on one of the trucks carrying the gas cylinders would, at the very least, be catastrophic to those within a considerable range of the vicinity.

This danger was highlighted on Sunday 16 June 1917, when men of the 4th Balloon Company were in the process of inflating their balloon in preparation for spotting for the 26th Yankee Division's artillery. The men had just broken for breakfast when German artillery shells rained down around them. Seconds later the Caquot balloon, which was only partially

Brigadier-General Benjamin D. Foulis, Chief of Air Service AEF.

sent to France. They were supposed to be ready to support the American divisions who were preparing for the great offensive. It was soon discovered, much to the anger of General Pershing, that the companies had only the basic rudiments of ballooning and would have to be sent to the French balloon schools for advanced training. This, of course, could not be done overnight – in fact it took nearly five months. Although these balloon companies carried out their duties with honour, great courage and fortitude, it was short-lived because they never entered the theatre of war until it was nearly over.

Brigadier-General Foulis was appointed Chief of Air Service, First Army, with

Colonel William Mitchell about to take off on an observation flight in a SPAD.

inflated, received a direct hit and exploded. Fortunately there were no serious casualties, but it decimated the area and dented the pride of the 4th Balloon Company, as they were the first American balloon company to lose their balloon – but they would not be the last.

While at the Front, living accommodation for the balloon companies was usually just two-man pup tents. Some of the companies spent over 250 days continuously living in the most horrendous of conditions and constantly on the move. After finishing their intensive training from the French, the companies were usually sent to the relatively quiet sectors where they carried out observations for artillery units and were eased into battle conditions.

On 31 January 1918, four more balloon companies – the 5th, 6th, 7th and 8th – were

Colonel Mitchell as his deputy. Brigadier-General Kenly was promoted to Major-General and appointed as Director of Military Aeronautics back in the United States. Colonel Mitchell continued to press for advancement of the Air Service, so much so, in fact, that Brigadier-General Foulis requested that Mitchell be appointed to Chief of Air Service, First Army, and that he himself become the Assistant Chief of Air Service under Brigadier-General Patrick. The request was granted in August 1918 and Mitchell, promoted to Brigadier-General, started to expand the Air Service rapidly. Within two months a Second Army was formed under Colonel Frank P. Lahm, and

just before the Armistice was signed, a Third Army was created.

The formative years of the United States Army Air Arm, or United States Air Service (USAS) as it was later to become known, were as part of the US Signal Corps, under the command of Lt-Col George O. Squier, and comprised 131 officers and 1,087 enlisted men. Squier, despite being a non-flyer, was ideally suited to the position after seeing air action when he had been the military attaché in London at the beginning of the war. Just after the American declaration of war, two of his subordinate officers, Captains Edgar Gorrel and Benjamin Foulis, drew up a proposed budget for the rapidly expanding Air Service.

A USAAS pilot learning to fly in Texas, USA in 1917, in Curtiss 'Jennies' JN-4s.

They drew the charts on large pieces of grocery wrapping paper acquired from a local store, and they showed a required budget of $600 million, a figure greater than that required to build the Panama Canal. Fortunately Squier had seen the war in Europe and realised that this figure was not going to be excessive, and persuaded the then Secretary of War, Newton D. Baker, that it was necessary, leaving him to successfully persuade members of Congress.

Squier realised that the Air Service was in desperate need of aircraft and facilities so he also persuaded the government to purchase a cotton field near San Antonio, Texas for the express purpose of training aviators. It was called Kelly Field, and by the end of the war 5,182 officers and 197,468 enlisted men had been trained there. He also presided over the acquisition of aircraft from Great Britain – the

de Havilland 4 – and arranged for them to be built in the United States under licence, but with the twelve-cylinder Liberty engine installed.

Of the number of officers initially in the Air Service, only twenty-six of them were in fact pilots; the remainder were engineers or administrative officers. Among the pilots were William Thaw and Raoul Lufbery, who had fought the Germans since 1914 and would do so until the end of the war. William Thaw had joined the *Légion Etrangère* at the beginning of the war as a private in Battalion C, 2nd Regiment. After serving with the *Légion Etrangère* for a while, Thaw transferred to *Escadrille D.6* or as a *soldat mitrailleur* (machine-gunner). But he wanted to fly, and after convincing the authorities that he had done some flying back in the United States, he was sent to the military aviation school at

Saint-Cyr late in 1915 where, after training, he was awarded his brevet. He was flying Caudron G.IIs with *Escadrille C.42* based at Nancy when word came through that an American unit was to be formed because of the increased number of American pilots joining up. Thaw immediately asked to be transferred, and within a very short time, because of his experience, was promoted to the rank of lieutenant-colonel in the USAS. In less than four years William Thaw had risen from private in the French Army to a lieutenant-colonel in the US Army and been given command of the 3rd Pursuit Group, US Air Service. A truly remarkable achievement, but then he was a rather remarkable man.

Raoul Gervais Victor Lufbery, on the other hand, had been born in France, the son of an American father and a French mother. His education was that of a French schoolboy, and after his mother died he was left in the care of his grandmother while his father returned to the United States. After many years of working his way around the world, he returned to the United States to find his father, but without success. He joined the US Army and fought in the Philippines against the natives, who were in revolt at that time. After three years Lufbery left the Army and went to Saigon, where he met and joined up with the French aviator Marc Pourpre as his mechanic. The two of them toured the Far East giving exhibitions, and finally ended up in Paris at the onset of the First World War. Raoul Lufbery then joined the Foreign Legion, but because of his experience and knowledge was almost immediately sent on detached duty to the *Service Aéronautique*. When his friend Pourpre was killed while trying to land in fog, Lufbery volunteered for training as a pilot and was posted to the Aviation School at Chartres. On graduating with the rank of sergeant he was posted to Bombardment Squadron No. 106, where he served with distinction until May 1916, when he was transferred to the *Escadrille Lafayette*.

Within a few months he had proved himself to be one of the most skilled pilots in the

Major Jean Huffer and Major Raoul Lufbery.

squadron, and had shot down six aircraft by the end of the year. By the beginning of 1917 he was among the highest-scoring pilots of the *Escadrille Lafayette*, and in August 1917 was commissioned *sous-lieutenant*, having been awarded the *Légion d'Honneur, Medaille Militaire, Croix de Guerre* with ten Palms and the British Military Medal. He was also becoming a household name in the United States. With the entrance of the United States into the war, great pressure was put on Lufbery to transfer to the United States Air Service, and with great reluctance he agreed. He transferred to the USAS on 10 January 1918 with the rank of major and was given temporary command of the 94th Pursuit Squadron.

Another American adventurer who came from the Foreign Legion was Eugene Bullard, one of the only two known black aviators to serve in the First World War – the other was *Feldwebel* Marcel Pliat, a Frenchman who fought with the Imperial Russian Air Service as an observer/gunner. Bullard, an ex-boxer, had been broke and penniless in Paris in 1914 and had joined the Foreign Legion's 170th Infantry. Later, when asked why he had joined the Foreign Legion, Bullard replied, 'Well, I don't rightly know, but it must have been more curiosity than intelligence.' This probably

Members of the Escadrille Lafayette. *L-R: Walter Lovell; Edmond C. Genêt; Raoul Lufbery and James McConnell.*

A SPAD V.II with its distinctive Seminole Indian insignia on the fuselage, being serviced by French mechanics. This aircraft was flown by Didier Masson, Raoul Lufbery and Kenneth Marr whilst in the Escadrille Lafayette.

summed up the reasons why many young Americans joined up to fight at the time.

At the end of 1916 Eugene Bullard asked to be transferred to the Flying Corps. After graduating as a pilot in July of 1917, he served with Spa.93 and later Spa.95 from August to November 1917, scoring one confirmed and one possible hit. It was just after his last mission that Bullard requested to leave the Flying Corps and that he be returned to the Foreign Legion's 170th Infantry. It was said that the discipline in the Flying Corps had proved too much for him and that that was the reason for his request, but the discipline in the Foreign Legion is legendary so it is hard to believe it was harsher in the Flying Corps. This, then, poses the question: Was it resentment towards his colour that forced Bullard to make the decision to leave the Flying Corps? What happened to Eugene Bullard after leaving is not recorded, nor is anything known about the other black aviator, Marcel Pliat.

Prior to the United States entering the war, a large number of Americans who wanted 'in' crossed the border into Canada and joined the Royal Flying Corps (RFC) and the Royal Naval Air Service (RNAS) under the guise of Commonwealth citizens. They had their primary training at Camp Borden, Ontario, before being shipped across the Atlantic for further training in Britain or France. From there they were dispatched to various squadrons in France. Later, just after America entered the war, 300 cadets selected from various American universities and about 800 enlisted men from the Signal Corps were sent to Camp Borden for training. They were called the Toronto Group. The initial training was not quite what the American volunteers had expected: they suddenly came up against the British military drill system and a discipline that was harsher than anything they had experienced before. But they realised there was a purpose behind it all and soon became accustomed to its rigours.

Ten squadrons were to be formed, and the flying training, because of the harsh winters in

Eugene Bullard – the only black American aviator in the First World War.

Canada, was split between Camp Borden in Ontario and Taliaferro Fields in Texas. Because of the lack of equipment and aircraft, only eight of the ten squadrons materialised: Nos. 17, 22, 27, 28, 139, 147, 148, and 183. Two of the squadrons, Nos. 17 and 148, were assigned to the Royal Flying Corps, although flown by American pilots. Nos. 22, 27, 139 and 147 were assigned to the 1st and 2nd Pursuit Groups of the USAAS, and No. 183 Squadron was later re-formed as part of the 278th Observation Squadron. The remaining squadron, No. 28 Pursuit Squadron, was assigned to the 3rd Pursuit Group.

Camp Borden – Canada.

L-R: Capt. Horace N. Niesen (pilot); Lt Miles W. Kresge (Observer) with ground crew Sgt Adolphson; Pvt Evans and Cpl Lambert, with their new DH.4 of the 278th Observation Squadron.

Another group of Americans who wanted to fly were selected from graduates from the Universities of Illinois, Texas and California and the School of Military Aeronautics at Princeton in August 1917. These volunteers were known initially as the 'Italian Detachment' (later known as the Oxford Group) as they were destined to be sent to Italy for flight training. Among the first of the Princeton students who went to Camp Borden for flight training was one James Forrestal, whose name was later to become synonymous with US naval aviation and after whom, many years later, one of the largest aircraft carriers ever built was named. The group's first stop, in fact, was England, where their orders were changed and they were sent to Oxford University for ground school training. After finishing the course, the Oxford Group were sent for primary, then advanced flight training

at various RFC bases in England. Then it was on to the School of Aerial Fighting at Turnberry in Scotland, where, upon graduating, they were given commissions to lieutenant and placed in a pool of RFC/RAF pilots ready for posting to squadrons on the Western Front.

Among this group of pilots and observers was Lt Elliott White Springs, the son of an extremely wealthy cotton-mill owner. Springs was picked out by Major William A. Bishop, VC, as an extremely promising fighter pilot, and in May 1918 he had him posted to No. 85 Squadron RFC under his command and tutelage. Despite his playboy image, Elliott White Springs learned quickly and soon became one of the squadron's top exponents of aerial fighting. By the end of June 1918 he had raised his tally to four, but on 27 June was shot down and injured. After spending some weeks in hospital he returned to his unit, only to find

No. 85 Squadron, RFC at Hounslow about to fly to France. L-R: Elliot White Springs; Horn; Longton; Larry Callaghan; Dymond; Thompson and Brown.

Lt Elliot White Springs wearing a relieved smile, after his Sopwith F1 Camel of No. 148th Squadron crashed after a German fighter had shot off one of his wheels and damaged his propeller.

Lt Elliot White Springs's Sopwith F1 Camel of 148th Squadron, USAS, being righted after he had crashed the aircraft during touchdown. Battle damage can be seen to the upper starboard wing and the propeller.

that he had been posted to the 148th Pursuit Squadron with a promotion to captain on 1 August 1918. Six more victories by the end of the month raised his score to ten and earned him the award of both the DSC (Distinguished Service Cross) from the British and the DFC (Distinguished Flying Cross) from the Americans. He was to end the war with a total of sixteen victories.

Elliott White Springs was to later write the classic First World War book *War Birds – The Diary of an Unknown Aviator*. It was later established that the 'unknown aviator' was in fact his friend, Lt John McGavock Grider, who had kept a diary of his and fellow pilots' lives up to the point of his death in June 1918. Elliott White Springs had been given the diary and continued to update it, embellishing it somewhat. Nevertheless, it gave an extremely accurate insight into the life of a First World War aviator.

The 93rd Pursuit Squadron was formed late in August 1917 at Jefferson Barracks, St Louis. It was formed out of the pick of the students who had just graduated and been immediately posted to Kelly Field for general army drill training. On completion of this the squadron moved to England, where the pilots and ground crews were assigned in groups to various Royal Air Force establishments for further training on engines and airframes. In May 1918, the squadron was regrouped and sent overseas to Issoudon, where they were greeted by their commanding officer, Major Huffer. Huffer, who had been assigned from the 94th Squadron, immediately arranged further training for the ground crews within the engine repair shops there, while the pilots attempted

The maintenance workshops at Kelly Field, Texas.

An FBA (Franco-British Aircraft) flying boat, showing the bombs in the racks fitted on the outside of the fuselage.

to get in some flying hours on French aircraft. In July 1918 the squadron moved to Vaucouleurs and into the war.

At the end of May 1917, a second Yale unit was formed under the leadership of Ganson Goodyear Depew of Buffalo, New York, who presented the idea to Admiral W.S. Benson who was Chief of Naval Operations (CNO) at the time. The twelve members of the unit were enlisted into the United States Naval Reserve Force (USNRF) and ordered to report to Lieutenant Wadleigh Capehart at Buffalo, New York. As was the practice at the time, most of the funding was from private sources. Equipment and a second-hand Curtiss flying boat were purchased. The Second Yale Unit's (or Aerial Coastal Patrol Unit No. 2, as it became known) existence was very nearly cut short when, on one of the first excursions of

the newly acquired Curtiss flying boat, it crashed, killing the instructor and so badly injuring the passenger that he was invalided out of the service and the war. Ganson Depew acquired another aircraft and flying instructor out of his own pocket and persuaded the naval authorities to give them another chance, which they did.

The trust that the Naval Board had bestowed upon them bore fruit, when in November all twelve passed the stringent tests required to acquire the 'Wings of Gold'. The final flying test was to take the Curtiss F flying boat up to 6,000 feet, cut the engine and glide down in a spiral, then land on the water and taxi to a point not less than twenty feet from a marker buoy. Three of the twelve students actually stopped with their aircraft's nose nestling against the buoy. The twelve were granted commissions as ensigns and five were posted overseas to Europe, six to NAS Pensacola and one to Washington DC. After arriving in Europe, the five new ensigns were posted to Moutchie, France for bombing instruction in French FBA flying boats. Later the same month, three of them were posted to RNAS Felixstowe, where they were introduced to the delights of the twin-engined F2A Flying Boat. The other two ensigns were assigned to the Northern Bombing Group (NBG) and carried out ferry flights of Caproni bombers from Italy over the Alps to northern France. These were hair-raising flights as the reliability of these aircraft was always being brought into question.

It was at Felixstowe in November 1917 that they took part in 'lighter stunt' experiments with the F2A Flying Boat. These were developed because of the need to carry out long-range reconnaissance flights over the North Sea. The distance from Felixstowe to the Danish coastline of Heligoland was 340 miles, and because the aircraft did not have this kind of range it could not spot German shipping making journeys northwards up the coast of Denmark. Wing Captain C.R. Sansom, RN, and Wing Commander Porte, RFC, had developed a 'lighter' (a type of barge) that could carry an F2A Flying Boat and be towed behind a destroyer at high speed. The 'lighter' was in fact a barge that settled quite low in the water and was a derivative of the lighter barges that were used to carry materials up and down the Thames. Three destroyers towing three lighters with F2As aboard left Felixstowe and proceeded across the North Sea to a point near the Dutch coast. The aircraft were offloaded from the lighters and then took off on patrol. The three aircraft flew along the coast to the Bight of Heligoland, then back across the North Sea to Felixstowe and returned safely. A number of flights were made using this system, and all were very successful.

Back in the United States the development of the USAS began to gain momentum as new roles for the Air Force were put forward. One of these, which had been put forward by Colonel Edgar S. Gorrell, president of the Stutz Motor Car Company, envisioned a strategic bombing campaign against the German industrial centres deep in the heart of Germany. Gorrell was not just an armchair officer; he had graduated from West Point in 1912, qualified as a pilot two years later and served under Pershing on the Mexican border. Pershing recognised him as a man who understood strategy and put him in charge of 'strategical aviation' – whatever that was deemed to be. Gorrell was sent to Europe as Assistant Chief of Staff of the Air Service, AEF, in October 1917, and after becoming aware of General Hugh Trenchard's concepts for strategic bombing he realised that not only would raids on the German industrial centres cause manufacturing problems, but the effect on German morale would also be a major factor.

The person who coined the phrase 'it sounds good in theory' must have been thinking of Gorrell's proposal, because on paper the idea certainly had merit, but from a practical point of view there were serious logistical problems. In France the idea was greeted with some scepticism, and it was estimated that it would take a raid of over 600 bombers to have any long-term effect on the German manufacturing economy. Training for these bombers would start in the United States on old Curtiss 'Jennies', and on completion of this, further training would have to be carried out in England on DH.4s or Handley Page bombers. The length of time required for both sets of training and the logistics of moving that amount of men and equipment around were horrendous. In addition to this it was realised that these bombers would need fighter escorts, and there were no fighters that had the range to fly to Germany and back escorting the bombers. This was a situation that was to be realised again during the Second World War. Gorrell's answer to this was that the bombers would afford their own protection by sheer weight of numbers and that the raids would be

Student pilot Sgt Joe Reed waits beside the wreckage of his Curtiss JN-6H after crashing due to engine failure.

carried out at night. This in itself was enough to squash the idea, but it was discussed in depth and ultimately dismissed. It was thought that the USAS had not developed enough to carry out such a mission. Indeed, it was thought that not even the Royal Flying Corps would consider such a raid.

The 1st Observation Squadron should have been the first American squadron to go into action, but there were no aircraft for them. Instead it was the 1st Aero Squadron, under the command of Major Ralph Royce, who arrived in France on 3 September 1917. Among the men who boarded the SS *Lapland* in New York were forty-six aviation cadets under the command of Major William O. Ryan. They were to move on to the 8th Aviation Instructional Centre at Foggia in southern Italy, which had recently been created for flight training.

This small, remote town had been selected by the Italian Ministry of Aviation as a training field for their expanding air force. But as more and more Americans came into the war, it was decided to use the airfield as a flight training facility for the Americans using Italian instructors. Initially it was thought that upwards of 1,000 pilots would graduate from the school, but as time progressed, budget cuts and an unusually high accident and drop-out rate resulted in only 411 pilots graduating.

The arrival in Italy of the first flight students was initially a novelty, for both the Americans and the local townspeople. The Americans' idea of a warm sunny Italy was soon dispelled by the damp weather that greeted them, together with the abundance of mosquitoes and flies. The latter disappeared as soon as the cold weather set in, but things did not improve for the students. Lt Sherwood Hubble, one of the first arrivals at Foggia, said it was a dirty,

US naval aviators training with the French at Avord-Cher, France.

filthy place where the majority of the townspeople cooked, ate and slept in one room together with their chickens and cows. He further stated that the one aim of the shopkeepers was to relieve the Americans of as much money as they could with grossly inflated prices.

Flying at the school started briskly enough, but as soon as the weather started to deteriorate the Italian instructors introduced the word *domani* (tomorrow) into the flight curriculum. And conditions never got any better. At the beginning of 1918 a detachment from the US Army Medical Corps descended upon the base and sprayed the area with a pesticide in an attempt to control the mosquito and fly population. The food on the base left a lot to be desired too, so much so in fact that a number of the students went into the town for their meals. Although a great deal of time and money was put into the training facility at Foggia, it never became the success that was

A French Dorand AR-1 of the 2nd Corps Aeronautical School at Chatillon-sur-Seine, France – 1918.

USAS aircraft at Issoudon airfield, France.

USAS mechanics repairing a battle damaged Sopwith Camel at Issoudon airfield, France on 20 March 1918.

A Salmson 2-A2 of the 90th Squadron, USAS, at Ourches, France, in July 1918.

expected of it.

The remainder of the cadet pilots were given further training as an observation squadron at the French Air Service school at Avord, and equipped with French Dorand AR-1s and 2s, SPAD XIs and the odd Sopwith. The aircraft were not well received by the squadron, who called them unaffectionately 'Antique Rattle traps', but they flew a number of missions with them, the first on 11 April 1918. Later the squadron moved to Issoudon for further training, but because of the camp's state of unreadiness they spent more time building and equipping the camp than flying. Major Royce went to Paris in an effort to arrange more flying training for his men. He sent the aviation mechanics to the various aircraft factories around Paris to increase their knowledge and improve their techniques.

In June of that year, much to their delight, the squadron was re-equipped with new Salmson 2-A2s. The squadron was then sent to the 1st Corps Aeronautical School at Amanty

for observer training. They were then able to use the Toul area that covered the 350-mile front from the English Channel to Switzerland. The area was chosen because it had been relatively quiet for some months and was deemed to be a good sector for breaking in pilots who had little or no combat experience. In January 1918, Major Royce returned to Amanty to take over as director of the school, as well as being the commanding officer of the 1st Aero Squadron. But still he had the problem of insufficient aircraft and spares. Early in 1917 the American aircraft industry, such as it was, had agreed to deliver over 20,000 aircraft. But it was obvious from the outset that they were totally incapable of producing such a vast number within such a short period of time. By the beginning of January 1918, the twelve companies capable of producing aircraft had only delivered a total of 800 aircraft, of which only 100 could be considered even to be used as combat aircraft.

On 21 February 1918, the US War

A Curtiss JN-4D being refuelled at Issoudon airfield in 1918.

Department announced that it was sending the first American-built warplanes, known as Curtiss 'Jennies' to the Western Front in France. In reality, the aircraft were British-designed DH.4s built by Curtiss, which in Europe were now considered to be obsolete. The first aircraft were shipped from Dayton, Ohio aboard a freighter that was later torpedoed off the Azores, so it was not until May 1917 that the first American-built DH.4s arrived in France. Out of a total of nearly 6,200 aircraft delivered to the USAS in France, only 1,200 (DH.4s) came from the United States. The remaining 5,000 came from France (SPADs, Salmsons, and Nieuports) and were ostensibly training aircraft. But in America things were starting to happen: manufacturers were getting their act together and starting to think ahead – especially the engine manufacturers.

The part being played by the few American airmen fighting in Europe was beginning to capture the imagination of the newspapers and the public. More and more young Americans were captivated by the stories of the daredevil fighter pilots in France, and consequently the Army was being inundated with requests for flight training. The government set up a commission headed by Brigadier-General Benjamin D. Foulis to look into flight training and sent them to Canada to see how the Canadians were producing their military aviators. On their return, the commission found that more than 18,000 Americans had volunteered for flight training. This may seem an overabundance of volunteer aircrew, but it has to be remembered that the lifespan of an aviator during the First World War was measured in weeks rather than months or years.

On 20 May 1918, the Airplane Division of the Army's Signal Corps was transferred from the control of the Signal Corps and came under the supervision of two different agencies controlled by the Secretary of War, the Bureau of Aircraft Productions and the Division of Military Aeronautics, and became the USAS

(United States Air Service). It was an unusual alliance, and one without precedent, so the choice of who was to head it caused problems. President Woodrow Wilson solved the problem by appointing the former head of Annaconda Copper, Mr John D. Ryan, as the Director of the Air Service and the Second Assistant Secretary of War.

Although the Americans now had plenty of training aircraft and volunteers, the one thing they were short of was airfields. It was decided by means of a reciprocal agreement between Britain, Canada and the United States that during the summer and autumn months the RFC (Royal Flying Corps) would train ten US squadrons in Canada, and in the winter squadrons would be trained at three airfields in Texas. The pilots carried out their primary training in both Canada and the United States and were awarded their 'wings', but as they had only flown training aircraft they were shipped overseas to carry out advanced combat training under French and British pilots before being allocated to their respective squadrons. The following signal was issued to all American servicemen who were to fight in France:

December 3, 1917 Stencil #694

WAR DEPARTMENT
Office of the Chief Signal Officer
Washington

INFORMATION SECTION – AIR DIVISION

The following confidential information is furnished for the use of the Army and Navy and authorised civilians in the service of the Government.
T.H. BANE
Lt. Col., Signal Corps

WARNING TO AMERICAN AVIATORS
Things to Avoid if Forced to Land behind German Lines

The following instructions in the form of a warning have been given to British Aviators. American Officers and Aviators should note them and appreciate their importance.

If you are unfortunate to be compelled to land behind the German lines, you may be agreeably surprised by the apparent hospitality and generosity of your welcome there. The German Officers will probably have you stay with them as their guest for a few days at one of their squadrons and will make you most comfortable. You will probably be extremely well entertained with the very best of everything they can offer. An abundance of good champagne from France will oil the wheels of conversation between the officers of the German Flying Corps, and one whom they will probably term a brother officer of the English Flying Corps. They will appear to be very good fellows, straightforward, cheerful and keen on the scientific side of flying, apart from their ordinary work with which they may say they are quite fed up. They will probably lead you to talk about the possibilities of aviation after the war, and profess little interest in aviation as actually applied to war. It may not take much wine to gladden your heart, and to induce you to lay aside your suspicions and reserve, and forget the guile which lies behind their artless questions.

And so unaccustomed as you are to this form of deceit, you may fall another victim to this clever combination of cunning and hospitality. But though they may succeed for the moment in making a favourable impression, you will afterwards have every reason to remember during this war the Germans have proved themselves to be a cruel and unscrupulous enemy, but they are sound financiers and have an eye to good investment. It does not cost them much to entertain you well, and even if they did expect to get an adequate return for their money in the form of information unwittingly imparted by you.

That's why they will give you all the

delights of the 'Carlton' and 'Savoy' with none of the regrets of an overdraft at Cox's and that is why you will be treated as a highly honored guest, instead of being half starved in one of the their now notorious prison camps, a treatment which is in fact only postponed until they have squeezed every ounce of useful information out of you. The work is done by experienced men. Quite unknown to yourself one or more of the seemingly irresponsible flying men are highly trained intelligence officers who will sift bits of useful information from your most brilliant 'bon mots' received with the keenest amusement and gratification.

On the other hand, different methods may be employed, though these are not so common with prisoners of the Flying Corps as with others. You may be browbeaten and ordered to disclose information under pain of suffering penalties, if you refuse. Remember this is only a ruse and they will not carry out their threats. It is more possible that they will respect you for your patriotism and discretion.

It is quite possible that you may be placed in a hut with an officer alleged to be an English prisoner, speaking English fluently and knowing many people in England well, and wishing to have news of everyone and everything, or perhaps he will ask no questions, relying only on your confidence. It will be difficult for you to believe that he is not a companion in misfortune, but this is a common trick of all intelligence services and a very profitable one.

Therefore, be on your guard and remember that in a show like this, it is impossible for any individual not at the head of affairs to say what is of use to the enemy and what is not. Remember that any information you may inadvertently have given may lengthen the war and keep you longer in Germany; may cost the lives of many Englishmen; may strain the country's resources even more than they are being strained at present. Don't think this is all imagination and needless caution. The need of it has been bought by experience. No careless or irresponsible feelings ought to weigh with us against anything we can do to hasten the conclusion of the war.

Chapter 4

January – September 1918:
American Squadrons Enter the War

At the beginning of January 1918, the first of the USAS squadrons arrived at the Air Service Concentration Barracks at St Maixent, France. The unit had been set up to evaluate and test the members of the various squadrons over a period of fifteen days, after which they were attached to various units at the Front.

There were still problems with aircraft production, however, and the situation was further aggravated when, on 7 February 1918, Brigadier-General Foulis received a cable from a Colonel S.D. Waldon of the production service of the Air Service in Washington stating that the desperately awaited fifty American-manufactured de Havilland DH.4s with the twelve-cylinder Liberty engine 'be retained in the United States for advanced training where they can be closely observed and the benefit of any troubles or necessary corrections be immediately given to the manufacturers. Do you approve?' To say that General Pershing was not pleased was an understatement. He was furious, and immediately cabled back: 'Send 45 of the DH.4s to the AEF immediately and keep five in the United States for training, observation and corrections.'

One week later, General Pershing received a cable from Colonel Waldon requesting confirmation of Pershing's demand and stating that if that were the case deliveries would start immediately. The only problem, Waldon explained, was that the aircraft would have no accessories, i.e. no radios, guns, gunsights or electrical apparatus for heating clothing. These additions would require a further two months. What he in fact would get was an aircraft with an engine and nothing else. Washington wanted the aircraft fully equipped and tested before they were sent to the AEF, but Pershing insisted that the only way to test these aircraft was in the conditions under which they would be expected to operate, and by pilots who understood the rigours, stresses and strains of combat aircraft.

It was becoming quite obvious that the aviation programme introduced by the US Congress on 24 July 1917 was naive in its approach. The idea that you could throw bodies and money into a war and win may have been feasible a few centuries back, but this was a war of machines and weapons the like of which had never been seen. What was also being recognised was that although manpower from the United States was a not a problem, aircraft, guns and ammunition were. There were more than 300,000 troops under General Pershing's command, and what had not been fully realised by the United States high command was that the war was spread across half of Europe and the demands for both men and armament in the battle areas were great. The lack of aircraft forced the Americans to place their observer graduates with French *escadrilles*, until such time that American aircraft were available.

Another major problem that was of great concern was the repair and refurbishment of the existing aircraft. Badly damaged aircraft were cannibalised to such an extent that on one squadron every aircraft had at least one part of one specific aircraft that had crashed. In another incident telephone wires were used to replace the flying wires on a number of aircraft. Problems were arising out of the poor-quality aviation fuel, poor magnetos and spark plugs, and lack of proper tools. Messages flashed backwards and forwards between the squadron engineering officers and headquarters, most of them very aggressive and angry. The frustration was felt by both parties, and increased efforts were made to resolve the problems. The message being sent back to the government in America was that the United States was not ready for war. It took a lot more than just money and men; it required appropriate organisational and logistical skills that were geared to a wartime situation, and this was totally new to the Americans.

In an attempt to placate General Pershing, the Army Chief of Staff, Peyton March, sent him a cable stating: 'Every effort is being made to meet your wishes, but manufacturing program of equipment, shipping, etc. has not advanced as rapidly as was hoped for in the beginning.' In fact, it was hardly advancing at all, and in the formative year it was left to the Allies to supply the aircraft and training for the AEF.

On 15 February 1918, three former members of the *Escadrille Lafayette N.471* – Lts Meredith Dowd, Joseph Gill and George Willard – were transferred and joined the *2ème Escadrille Américaine*, which was renumbered *Esc.N.471* and became known unofficially as the Second *Escadrille Lafayette*. According to some historians, the squadron accounted for six enemy planes and one balloon, but little else is known

about it. How or why it was given the same number as the original *Escadrille Lafayette* is not known, but it is thought it may have been initiated by the three pilots, Dowd, Gill and Willard, who were transferred to the squadron.

There is one other explanation, however: the *Camp Retranche de Paris* (CMP) *Escadrilles* numbered from 461 to 470, and the original N.471 was created out of increasing demands to defend Paris. It is an accepted fact that both sides were desperate for pilots, as the air crew loss rate was extremely high. It was because of this that the *2ème Escadrille Américaine* had been created, and fifteen other pilots were assigned to the squadron. The ground crews and support personnel were all French, and the squadron was put under the command of Lt Le Comte Sanche de Gramont as part of *Groupe de Chasse 21*, which was under the command of Colonel LeClerc.

The squadron formed up at Le Bourget Field and began the task of being 'Defenders of Paris', with particular attention being paid to the night raids being carried out by German bombers. The aircraft supplied to the squadron were Nieuport 27s, used at the time as flight trainers. The mechanics soon fitted night-landing flares on the lower wings, but these proved to be totally useless. Their tireless patrols were barely more than just a 'flexing of muscles', and the Germans continued to advance, so much so, in fact, that the squadron had to relocate to Château-Thierry, some thirty-seven miles away. Things were now so desperate that orders went out to the pilots to fly at low level along the German trenches and shoot everything that moved. This tactic, of course, was bound to take its toll in casualties, and the first to fall was the commanding officer, Comte de Gramont, on 3 July 1918. His place was taken by Lt Walter Avery, USAS, who soon proved his worth by taking part in one of the fiercest ground-strafing missions, on 14 July, Bastille Day. For nearly two months the squadron flew virtually continuous strafing missions against the German ground forces, and by the middle of July the tide had been stemmed. The

German advance had been halted and they had begun their retreat. The threat to Paris was over and the squadron was virtually disbanded, the Americans being sent to various fighter squadrons. The Second *Escadrille Lafayette* was no more, but it had proved its worth.

There was another unit assembled on similar lines: the British 2nd Army Corps, designated the 183rd Flight Detachment. The squadron had started life as one of ten squadrons trained by the RFC in Canada that were collectively known as the 'Toronto Group'. After extensive training both in Canada and in Texas, they were sent to France for advanced combat flying instruction. On completion of their training, ten of the American pilots were assigned to become a 'flight detachment' of the British 2nd Army Corps based at Luxeuil-les-Bains.

The airfield was already a legendary place: it has been the original home of the *Escadrille Lafayette* and the base from which the Zeppelin sheds at Friedrichshafen were bombed. Equipped with obsolete Sopwith 1½ Strutters, the 183rd were no match for the German fighters, so they were only able to operate as

observation aircraft when there were no German aircraft in the area. This, of course, was not always possible, and there were the inevitable casualties. The pilots became impatient for new aircraft, but the 183rd Flight Detachment were just a memory in the minds of the hierarchy until just before the St Mihiel offensive, when, under the command of Lt Hughes, they were merged with the 258th Observation Squadron. Within two months twenty-four new Salmson 2-A2s arrived.

A number of pursuit squadrons belonging to the 1st Pursuit Group became operational at the beginning of 1918: the 95th Pursuit Squadron, 94th Squadron, 27th Squadron and the 147th Squadron. Although the 95th was the first to arrive in France, it was discovered that none of the pilots had training on the machine-guns, so the honour of being the first into action went to the 94th. The squadron, later commanded by Captain Eddie Rickenbacker, had as its emblem the famous 'Hat-in-the-Ring'.

The 95th were in action only a matter of weeks later. The squadron had arrived at the small village of Villeneuve-les-Vertus on 18

Lt Reed Chamber of the 94th Aero Squadron (6 victories).

Members of the 94th Aero Squadron (Hat-in-the-Ring). L-R: Lt Joe Eastman; Capt. Jim Meissner; Capt. Eddie Rickenbacker; Capt. Reid Chambers and Lt Thorne Taylor.

February 1918 under the command of Captain James E. Miller. Miller had been a former staff officer with General Pershing at his headquarters in Paris and had been in charge of Advanced Field No. 5 when assigned to command the 95th in place of its temporary commander, Raoul Lufbery. The squadron proceeded on to the airfield of Villeneuve which was some four kilometres from the village itself. The aircraft assigned to the squadron were Nieuport 28s, and they were awaited with great anticipation. Then, on 6 March, they arrived – *sans* guns.

Two American pilots, Majors Davenport Johnson and Millard Harmon, both on temporary assignment to *Groupement Menard* which was based at Villeneuve, offered to take Captain Miller on patrol over the lines. On the morning of 9 March 1918, flying a SPAD borrowed from the French group and accompanied by Harmon and Johnson, also flying borrowed French aircraft, Miller took off on patrol. Harmon soon suffered engine trouble and had to return, leaving only Johnson and Miller. Just outside Craonne they sighted a flight of German two-seater aircraft and attacked. The inexperience of Miller resulted in his being shot down and killed. Johnson's guns had jammed, forcing him to break off the attack, but he had not warned Miller that the two-seaters were armed at both front and rear. The result was that while attempting to attack from behind, Captain Miller was met with a hail of bullets. Captain Davenport Johnson was ordered by General Mitchell to take over command of the 95th on 20 March 1918.

This incident highlighted the lack of gunnery and aerial combat training, and although the 95th had had some training, it was obviously not enough. Firing at a moving target was one thing, but firing at a moving, twisting target that fired back was something entirely different. The squadron was ordered immediately to Cazeaux for increased target training, but it was soon realised that there was no substitute for the real thing, and that was to prove costly in both lives and aircraft – for both sides.

Early in January, Brigadier-General Foulis had received a cable from the War Department informing him that they had implemented a plan to train air crews in aerial gunnery and that facilities would be available by 15 May 1918. This was to be in the shape of aircraft with target-towing facilities and two-seat aircraft with movable and synchronised guns. He was also told that a school for observers was to be opened at Kelly Field, San Antonio, Texas, on 1 March, together with a bombing school at Houston, Texas. In addition to this a pursuit school was to be opened at Lake Charles, Louisiana. Foulis realised from past experience that if he was to wait for these programmes to be implemented, not only would there be no one to fight in France, but the war would probably end before they materialised. This was a prime example of the lack of understanding between the War Department in the United States and the men fighting the war in France. It was because of this that Foulis activated his own programme at Cazeaux.

Slowly but surely, the 95th Pursuit Squadron, after completing its gunnery course at Cazeaux, regained its morale and started to make its mark. Then, in June, Major Johnson

Officers of the 1st Observation Group. L-R: A.J. Cole, CO of the 1st Aero Squadron; Lt Winchester, Intelligence Officer; Steward Bird, Chief Observer and Operations Officer 50th Aero Squadron; Lt Stuck, Chief Observer and Operations Officer 12th Aero Squadron; Dan Morse, CO 50th Aero Squadron and Stephen Noyes, CO 12th Aero Squadron.

Lt Everett Cook, CO 91st Observation Squadron standing beside his personal SPAD X.III, although the squadron used Salmsons.

was replaced by Captain David McK. Peterson, a former member of the *Escadrille Lafayette*. (Peterson stayed in the post for four months before going home; his replacement was Captain John Mitchell, who had served as Flight Commander with the 95th Pursuit Squadron.) The squadron pilots were sent on leave to Paris and, while on their way back to the squadron, were diverted to Colombey-les-Belles, and from there to Toul, where they joined up with their ground crews and the 94th Pursuit Squadron.

The same gunnery problem had been experienced by members of the 1st Corps Observation Group when, during their final days of training at Neufchâteau, they were invited to visit a French Breguet bombing group based nearby. Major Royce, the school's commanding officer, and also commanding officer of the 1st Aero Squadron, had made arrangements for the students to go on

bombing raids with the squadron to gain experience. The pilots of the bombers assumed that all the students had been trained as gunners, and because of the language difficulty confirmation was never established. On one particular raid on Saarbrücken on 25 February 1918, the bombers were attacked by German Albatros fighters while over the target. Of the eight bombers on the raid, three of them carried American observers from the school. During the attack by the fighters it was soon realised by the French pilots that their observers had had no combat training whatsoever and they had to flee for their lives. One student, Lt Stephen W. Thompson, managed to acquit himself handsomely by shooting down one of the Albatros fighters. He admitted later that he was terrified at the time, and his legs were shaking so much that he had to brace them against the fuselage. The French pilots were not at all pleased.

This situation only compounded the frustrations the Army's High Command in Europe were experiencing. The German Army had moved its Eastern Front troops westwards after the Russian Army had collapsed in November 1917. At the beginning of 1918 the German Army consisted of 192 divisions of battle-hardened troops, as opposed to forty-nine British, fifty-three French and five American divisions. The American troops up to this point had had insufficient training and were desperately short of supplies. General Pershing realised that to stop the German advance there had to be a concerted effort by the Allies, and he passed control of the US Army into the hands of *Generalissimo* Foch as Supreme Commander.

The German Army made its thrust towards the Allied lines in March 1917, and by June had opened up a gap between the British and the French. Although they continued to make ground, the Germans failed to break the British lines. The main thrust then moved toward the French lines along the Aisne River; the French had failed to destroy some of the bridges and the Germans were able to cross virtually unopposed. On 29 May they captured Soissons, and a week later had reached the Marne River. Then, for some inexplicable reason, the Germans halted their advance, apart from a number of brief but intense battles along the Allied lines. The lull enabled the Allies to regroup and rearm, and when the next push came, it came from the Allies at Château-Thierry and was, to some, the turning point of the war.

Slowly but surely the number of aircraft increased, as did the spares and tools, until it reached an almost acceptable level. Most of the observers, who had graduated from the school at Amanty and had been 'farmed' out to the various French *escadrilles* and other squadrons, returned to form the nucleus of the 1st Observation Group. The group comprised the 1st, 12th and 88th Observation Squadrons and was based at Francheville, twenty-five miles from the front line.

The 88th Observation Squadron, together with the 90th and 91st Observation Squadrons, had arrived in Liverpool in November 1917 from Texas aboard the Cunard liner *Orduna,* together with 9,000 other troops. Their journey then continued via a cross-Channel steamer from England and then across France aboard a rattling, decrepit French train packed twenty-four to a carriage to Barisey-le-Cote, and then, by means of a five-kilometre march, to Colombey-les-Belles. The cramped conditions aboard the liner and the train were alleviated somewhat by the less cramped conditions of Colombey-les-Belles' finest hotel/livery stable. The 88th's commanding officer, Lt Mahan, immediately embarked the squadron on building their own barracks, forming the basis of what was to become the 1st Air Depot. The 91st Observation Squadron then moved on to Amanty to equip itself with aircraft, then on to its base at Gondreville to take up the task of an Army Observation Squadron. Although not as glamorous as the image of the fighter pilots, observation was nevertheless one of the most dangerous aspects of flying during the war. Their task was to observe troop movements and gun positions far behind the enemy's lines, up to 20 miles in some cases and at a height of around 15,000 feet. It required some of the best pilots and observers in the USAS, and by the end of the war the squadron had lost eight pilots and eleven observers, but had accounted for 21 enemy aircraft – not bad for an observation squadron. Also arriving from England late in July, where they had been with the repair and maintenance section at the Central Flying School, were the 104th Observation Squadron. They arrived at St Maixent where Lt Clearton Reynolds took charge. I say squadron, but they only had one aircraft and one pilot: Reynolds. The remainder of the squadron was made up of mechanics. Lt Reynolds and Sgt Dube ferried a Salmson to their new base at Luxeuil-les-Bains while the rest of the squadron went by motor transport. At the end of August, 99th Observation Squadron pilots, who themselves had only just arrived in France, ferried in 18 Salmson 2-A2 aircraft, but there were still no pilots for the 104th. Time was spent checking out each aircraft, after which Reynolds carried out test flights. The biggest problem that faced the squadron then, was that not only did they not have sufficient pilots, but the aircraft had arrived far too late and the war was rapidly coming to a conclusion.

The squadron did see some action, however, when, together with the 24th Army Observation Squadron – who, like the 104th, had been in England in the servicing and maintenance sections – it was moved up to the Front to Souilly. The two squadrons were there when the push in the St Mihiel sector came, and a number of the new and very inexperienced pilots who had only just arrived at the squadrons were lost. But after the initial surge, the observation flights turned into what can only be described as pleasure flights, which ended with the signing of the Armistice. The 99th Observation Squadron, after having delivered the 104th Salmsons, had to wait for the delivery of their own, and by the time they arrived, so had the bad weather. The result was that they never saw any action.

Both the 43rd and the 69th Balloon Companies were involved in the action at St Mihiel. The 43rd initially took a terrible pounding when the Germans found an Allied ammunition dump and rained Allied shells down upon them for a number of hours. When the push started and the Germans retreated, it was so rapid that the company only managed to make two ascents during the battle. Their one claim to fame was that they heard the last shell from either side pass overhead on 11 November 1918. The 69th, on the other hand, supported the 42nd Infantry Division and during the battle lost two balloons but no men. It was a similar story for all the balloon companies, and although they did not get the recognition they thoroughly deserved, they, like many others, played a significant part in the war.

Another squadron arrived in late June, the 9th Night Observation Squadron commanded by Lt Thomas Box. When Box arrived at Amanty, he brought with him some of the pilots who had served with him on the 88th Observation Squadron: Gardiner Daily, Harold Merrill, Willard Thomas, Leslie Thompson, Harry Grainger and Philip West. Box's first communication with headquarters was: 'It will be impossible for us to do much until we are assigned some hangar space.' Space was offered to them in the 96th Bombardment Squadron hangars and six Breguets were ferried in, three from Colombey and three from the 90th Observation Squadron. At the end of the August 1918 the squadron moved to Vavincourt, and by this time they had scrounged an additional six aircraft, bringing the total to twelve. Lt Box had managed to acquire the aircraft, but he had only three pilots and four observers, so he spent time going around other airfields, managing only to acquire a few more pilots. The ground crews worked countless miracles in preparing the aircraft for the armada that was to support the St Mihiel offensive, and when it happened the 9th had eighteen aircraft in the air.

Two other observation squadrons arrived, and the three of them were formed into the 1st Corps Observation Group under the command of Lt-Col Lewis H. Brereton, who later became a general during the Second World War. (At the beginning of January 1918, Colonel Billy Mitchell had become Chief of the Air Service, 1st Corps. There existed a strained relationship between Mitchell and Brereton at the time, which General Pershing knew about, but although strained, Mitchell's appointment seemed, if anything, to heighten their professionalism and their respect for each other.) Within two months all squadrons were in action, and the glamorous image of the fighter pilot, created by the media back in the United States, was suddenly stripped away to reveal the brutal reality of war and death.

The Toul sector, however, was the ideal place for the squadrons to gain combat

The body of Lt Quentin Roosevelt, son of the former US President Teddy Roosevelt, lying beside the remains of his aircraft after being shot down.

experience, because although there was action, there were no frantic air battles taking place such as those being experienced in other sectors. But this was not to say it was not hazardous, and there were casualties, among them Lieutenant Quentin Roosevelt, the son of former US President Teddy Roosevelt. Quentin Roosevelt was one of those rare characters who, although coming from distinguished parents, possessed great charm and never lived on his name. His name, however, was to cause him some problems; his superiors tried to keep him away from the Front, until he insisted that he be treated the same as his fellow pilots.

Quentin Roosevelt died on 14 July 1918 while on a reconnaissance mission, when he and several other pilots from the 95th Pursuit Squadron were attacked by a force of German fighter aircraft. During the fight his aircraft received numerous hits from a Fokker D-7 flown by *Feldwebel* Christian Donhauser of *Jasta* 21. Many reports said that it was *Feldwebel* Karl Thom (later to be awarded the coveted *Pour le Mérite*) who had shot Roosevelt down, but it was established later from German records that it was indeed Donhauser, adjutant of *Jasta* 11 (von Richthofen's former squadron). According to German reports at the time, Lieutenant Roosevelt suffered two bullet wounds to the head, then his aircraft caught fire and crashed. The Germans later dropped a note saying that they had 'buried

him with full military honours after he had showed conspicuous bravery against highly experienced adversaries'. His grave was discovered three weeks later, by Capt. Hamilton Coolidge and a team of engineers from the 303rd Engineer Battalion, when the Allied front line had moved forward towards the Vesle River.

Lt-Col Brereton took advantage of the relatively quiet Toul sector and organised a training scheme that enabled his air crews to train with the infantry divisions that were located in the area. Conversely, the infantry divisions trained with the air crews in accumulating intelligence information and passing it back to the branch intelligence officer and his team of four. They had been integrated into the 1st Observation Group by the Chief of the Air Staff, because he dreamed of a time when the whole sector would be under the control of the Americans and would have to rely on nobody but themselves. In the meantime, the USAS was entering into an area of warfare they had never experienced before, so the 1st Observation Group came under the tactical control of the French XXXVII Corps.

Major Ralph Royce, as group operations officer and also commander of the 1st Aero Squadron, organised the first assignments for the squadrons. They flew long-range photographic missions and reconnaissance flights, and 'spotted' for the heavy artillery units, the first mission being with the 26th Yankee Division. However, quiet as the Toul sector was, these missions were not without their moments of danger, as there were reports of the aircraft being fired upon by their own side. This rude awakening to the realities of war served to highlight not only the need for co-operation and training between the various sections of the Army, but also the dangers of flying reconnaissance missions.

Royce continued to prepare the missions for the group's three squadrons – 1st, 12th and 88th (the latter had moved to Amanty under Major Harry B. Anderson to begin their observer's course) – dividing each squadron into three flights of six aircraft each and keeping at least six aircraft on alert at all times. Even at this stage Royce had the pilots and ground crews for the squadrons, but hardly any aircraft. The only aircraft available at this time were French Dorands, and they were fast becoming obsolete. After planning the first mission over enemy lines, Royce volunteered to do it himself, and on 15 April 1918 he carried out the first reconnaissance mission over German lines.

The use of aerial photography, although in its infancy, was regarded as being of great importance, and because the 1st Aero Squadron were the only ones with any sort of experience, they were given the initial task of co-ordinating with the 51st Artillery Brigade Headquarters. The 12th Observation Squadron was used for infantry liaison in the quiet sector east of Luneville with the 42nd Division, an unenviable role. It meant that pilots and observers had to fly their aircraft close to the ground, leaving themselves open as targets for everything that could fire a bullet or a shell. It was also a time when the use of display panels, correction of artillery ranging and aircraft recognition were practised.

In May 1918 two obsolete Sopwith $1^{1}/_{2}$ Strutters were assigned to the squadron and flown in by two delivery pilots. The first one landed without incident, but the second pilot misjudged his landing and careered into Major Anderson's Cadillac staff car. Anderson was not well pleased. Aircraft in his eyes were deemed to be an expendable item; staff cars were not – especially his! The Sopwith repaired, the squadron moved to Ourches and started reconnaissance flights of the sector, giving support to the artillery of the 26th and 77th Divisions and taking photographs of the Toul sector. The area was still relatively quiet, giving the squadron pilots time to get accustomed to flying over combat areas and practising manoeuvres. An attack on one of the Sopwiths on 5 July, when it was attacked by two Albatros Scouts but driven off after suffering only minor damage, heralded an end to inactivity in the sector.

The Allies counter-attacked at Château-Thierry on 18 July 1918, and all the observation squadrons, now equipped with a variety of aircraft, came into their own. Their almost hourly reports of enemy movements and positions to the American 4th Division and the VIth French *Armée*, were instrumental in playing a major part in this turning point of the war. All along the Front British, French and American divisions made their push and, supported by the RAF and the USAS, started to drive the Germans back. The bitter fighting made slow progress at first, but then it gathered momentum and, as one observer put it, 'the sky was black with Sops'.

The 1st and 12th Squadrons moved to Coincy, while the newly blooded members of the 88th Squadron came face to face with the horrors of war when their squadron moved up to Ferme-de-Grèves. The whole area had been turned into a wasteland pitted with craters and shell holes and littered with the bodies and remains of soldiers and their equipment. With the move to Ferme-de-Grèves the 88th Squadron became part of the 3rd Corps Observation Group.

The 94th also had their fair share of the bloody nature of war. Formed at Kelly Field on 20 August 1917, the same time as the 95th Pursuit Squadron, the 94th was commanded almost from the word go by Major Jean Huffer, who had been born in France of American parents. A fluent French speaker, he had served with the Lafayette Flying Corps with distinction and was given command of the 94th Pursuit Squadron while the pilots were in their final days of training at Issoudon. Among the pilots at Issoudon were Eddie Rickenbacker, Oscar Gude, Joe Eastman and Douglas Campbell, who, on completion of their course, were sent to Cazeaux for gunnery instruction, while the remainder of the squadron moved to Villeneuve. Prior to the arrival of the squadron at Villeneuve, Huffer arranged for a number of former *Escadrille Lafayette* pilots to be assigned to him including Hall, Lufbery, Marr, Peterson, Chapman, Cunningham, Davis, Loomis and Winslow. The addition of these highly experienced pilots to his squadron gave a tremendous boost to the new members, and their confidence showed on patrol.

The squadron's arrival at Villeneuve was not without problems, the main one being that there were no aircraft for them. They were told that the pilots would have to go to Colombey and Villacoublay to collect Nieuport 28s, but fortunately the 95th Squadron was pulled out to go to Cazeaux and seven of the aircraft were taken over by the 94th. But even then the aircraft were not ready for combat and ground crews worked around the clock to prepare them. The first observation flight, on 19 March, had to be carried out with French escort fighters from the *Groupement Menard* because the American aircraft had no machine-guns, but before long this had been rectified and the squadron was fully operational.

On 21 March the Germans opened up a massive offensive along the Front from the English Channel to Reims, with the result that every British and French squadron along the

L-R: Lt Oscar Gude; Eddie Rickenbacker, Alan Winslow and Major Raoul Lufbery.

1st Lt Alan Winslow standing beside his first victory, an Albatros D.V flown by Uffz. Simon of Jasta 64.

Original members of the Escadrille Lafayette *with pilots of the 4th Bombardment Group.*

A Fokker D.VII of Jagdstaffel 65 *flown by* Ltn. *Heinz von Beaulieu-Marconnay, after being forced down by aircraft of the 95th Pursuit Squadron, USAS.*

Front was on full defensive alert. The 94th Squadron was moved from Villeneuve to Epeiz as a back-up, and within two days of the move they were in action. Then suddenly, on 7 June, without reason and much to the chagrin of the squadron members, Huffer was replaced by Major Kenneth Marr and given command of the 93rd Pursuit Squadron. It was rumoured that he had somehow upset the Air Service hierarchy, but no reason was ever given.

The 94th suffered its first loss on 3 May 1918 when, while on patrol over Autrepierre, Lt Charles Chapman, a former member of the Lafayette Flying Corps, attacked five German aircraft, bringing down one before he himself was shot down in flames. For this he was awarded a posthumous DSC.

Raoul Lufbery continued to increase his score, but on 19 May 1918 a lone German Rumpler flown by *Unteroffizier* Kirschbaum

with his observer, *Leutnant* Schibe, had got past the French anti-aircraft batteries and prowled over the airfield.* The Rumpler had been engaged briefly by Lt Oscar Gude, who had exhausted his ammunition from six very long-range passes. Raoul Lufbery, who was in the squadron office at the time, jumped into his Nieuport and gave chase. After a brief skirmish, Lufbery's aircraft was seen to career all over the sky, then flip onto its back. As the aircraft rolled on its back, a figure and a cushion were seen to fall from the cockpit and crash into the garden of a nearby cottage. The aircraft then caught fire and crashed into a nearby field. By the time the first of the squadron members arrived, the body of Lufbery had been reverently laid out by the peasants. The only external mark on his body was a bullet hole through his left hand. It was decided after a great deal of investigation that Lufbery had

---

*The two Germans in the Rumpler were shot down later that day by French fighters. The crew was captured, and they spent the remainder of the war in a prisoner camp.

Major Raoul Lufbery in the cockpit of his Nieuport 27. To the left are Captain Soubiran and Lt Didier Masson – all members of the Escadrille Lafayette.

climbed into the cockpit of his aircraft and not fastened his seat belt. During the skirmish that followed, it is thought that the control wires in his aircraft were severed, with the result that he lost control. As the aircraft rolled on to its back, Lufbery fell out and plunged several hundred feet to the ground.

He was given a large military funeral attended by some of the highest-ranking officers of the French and American air services. His coffin was borne by Huffer, Peterson and Marr, together with three French pilots. After the funeral, a report regarding Lieutenant Gude's part in the incident was sent to Colonel John Mitchell, who said: 'For his performance I sent the pilot to the rear.' Lt Oscar Gude was transferred from the 94th on 11 July and posted to the 93rd Pursuit Squadron.

Chapter 5

US Naval Aviation (US Naval Air Service) at War

T he sometimes forgotten side of First World War aviation started to make its presence felt when, on 3 July 1918, the United States Navy raised the American flag over the RAF base at Killingholme, Lincolnshire, making NAS Killingholme the largest US naval air station in Europe.

Just prior to taking over the station, a

Handing over ceremony of Killingholme Air Station to the US Navy.

Zeppelin was reported to be heading for the area and two of the American pilots, Ensign Ashton 'Tex' W. Hawkins and Lt (jg) G. Francklyn Lawrence, took off in their H.16 flying boat to intercept. After flying through heavy rain and strong winds, Tex Hawkins climbed the aircraft through the clouds to 10,000 feet. There was no moon that night and the two Americans scoured the star-filled skies for a sign of the Zeppelin, but to no avail. After several hours of chasing shadows, they brought the aircraft down through the heavy overcast and into heavy fog. Hopelessly lost, they cruised at wave-top height until they spotted a line of trawlers heading out to sea. Assuming that the trawlers were going out to sea, they reversed the course the trawlers were taking and headed towards the coast. When a rock breakwater loomed in front of them, they hopped over and landed in a harbour. As they taxied towards the shoreline, a seaplane ramp loomed up in front of them, with a black cavernous hangar situated at the end of it. An amazed RNAS ground crew hauled the H.16 up the ramp, whereupon a Royal Navy officer asked them how the devil they had managed to find the base in such filthy weather. Tex Hawkins glanced at his co-pilot, and with a wink replied, 'The one thing they taught us to do in flight training was to navigate,' grinning with obvious relief.

On 5 June 1917, the first contingent of United States naval aviators had arrived at Pauillac, France, aboard the converted collier USS *Jupiter* (AC-3). Three days later a second contingent aboard another converted collier, USS *Neptune* (AC-8), landed at St Nazaire, France. The two groups were under the command of Lieutenant Kenneth Whiting and comprised seven officers and 122 enlisted men, none of whom had any aviation training or experience. Whiting immediately negotiated with the French for accommodation and training for one of the groups, as it was his intention to get his aviators into the fray as quickly as possible. With agreements reached he headed for London with the other group and a

meeting with Admiral William S. Sims, Commander US Naval Forces Europe, to tell him what he had done. Lt Whiting arranged with the Royal Navy that the US naval pilots would be sent to various RNAS stations for training after finishing their introductory course at Calshot.

The arrival at the RNAS stations came as bit of a shock to the Americans, who were used to a rather relaxed form of discipline. The expression 'running a tight ship' took on a whole new meaning when they came up against the rigid discipline of the British Navy. Two ensigns, John Vorys and Albert Sturtevant, were posted to RNAS Felixstowe under the command of Lt-Cdr O.H.K. Maguire. Sturtevant's large red moustache was the first thing to go, as in the Royal Navy one was only allowed either to be clean-shaven or to have a full beard. The two ensigns immediately addressed themselves to fitting in with the regime and were soon part of the complement of sixty RNAS officers and ratings that manned the station.

Back in London, Admiral Sims immediately took to Whiting's eagerness and sent him back to the United States with a request that Washington establish a training station at Mount-Lacanau, near Bordeaux. This was granted and the training establishment was set up, together with operational stations at St Trojan, Dunkirk and Le Croisic. Promoted to lieutenant-commander, Whiting was replaced by a more senior officer, Captain Hutchinson Cone, USN, and returned to the United States in January 1918, after having organised the setting up of US naval air stations throughout Europe in conjunction with the Royal Air Force. Through Whiting, the US Navy now had in place the makings of a very respectable aviation force.

One American sailor who remembered his first introduction to flying in the Navy was Ensign Joe C. Cline. He had enlisted in the United States Navy on 3 April 1917 as a Landsman for Quartermaster (Aviation). He was sent to NAS Pensacola with a number of other eager student aviators for flight training;

Aerial view of Brest, France. USNAS Brest can be seen bottom centre.

unfortunately there was no provision for such a large contingent of students at ground school or otherwise. For three weeks the group was drilled and indoctrinated into the naval way of life. This in itself was no hardship for Joe Cline, as he had spent four years in the Illinois Naval Militia prior to joining the Navy. Then, quite suddenly, the group was posted overseas to France. They boarded the USS *Neptune* at Baltimore and, with the destroyers USS *Perkins* and USS *Jarvis* as escorts, headed across the Atlantic towards France.

Two days later the group headed for the then small fishing village of Brest and took over what had once been the barracks of Napoleon's soldiers. In the meantime Lt Whiting had returned from Paris with an agreement that the French would train them as

pilots and supply them with aircraft, engines, fuel, armament and bombs. The group was loaded into trucks and driven to Tours, the home of the *Ecole d'Aviation Militaire de Tours*. They were arranged into groups of eight and each group was assigned to one instructor. One leather flying coat, one pair of goggles and one crash helmet was given to each group, and these were passed from one student to another as and when he came to fly in the school's Caudron G.3. There was one minor problem, however: the French instructors did not speak any English and the American students did not speak any French. It was resolved by having paste cards with a line drawn down the middle, with English on one side and French on the other. After each flight the instructor would point out the mistakes on the paste cards while

The result of a bad landing in the sea for one of the US Naval Air Service flying boats.

verbally berating the student in French. Two thirds of the group managed to solo after only five hours of instruction, so it said something for the ability of the French instructors and the ingenuity of the American students.

On completion of the course, the students were sent to *Ecole d'Aviation Maritime de Hourtin* based on a small lake outside Bordeaux. It was here that the Americans received their preliminary seaplane training on FBAs. After one month, the students were sent to the *Ecole d'Aviation de St Raphael* in the south of France. Here the students were taught to fly a variety of seaplanes, carry out bombing and gunnery courses, and carry out a number of water landings on the sea. Just four months after arriving in France, and with thirty-one hours and fifty-two minutes of flying time

behind him, Joe Cline received his French brevet. He was later posted to Le Croisic to join pilots of the First Aeronautic Detachment.

At the small village of Le Croisic by the Loire River, the small US naval air station based there had been operational since October 1917. The building of the station had commenced on 26 July 1917 and had been built using nineteen German prisoners-of-war. But it was not until 29 October that the base was activated, with the arrival from the United States of three ensigns (two of whom were pilots), thirteen enlisted men and eleven observers. The first flight from the base was made on 18 November, and the US Navy had their first taste of action. They were called to investigate the sighting of a German submarine off the coast, and Ensign Kenneth Smith, the pilot, Ensign Frank Brady, observer, and machinist W.M. Wilkinson clambered aboard their newly arrived Tellier flying boat and, with a bomb under each wing, took off. Dawn had only just broken, but by the end of the day they still had not returned. As soon as it was light the following day the other flight crews were scrambled to look for them. They had no luck, and it was not until late afternoon the following day that the aircraft and its crew were spotted by a French torpedo boat, tossing about on the rough seas some fifty miles from land. They had run out of fuel after misjudging the length of time they had been in the air and had to touch down on the water and ride out the bad weather. The accident report filed by the crew is now part of US naval history:

Thursday, Nov. 22, 1917.

Weather conditions were not ideal for flying, clouds being very low and quite a sea running.

After leaving Le Croisic, we started south steering course 195. On reaching Ile d'Yeu, found our drift to be considerably to the East. After picking up Point Breton on Ile d'Yeu, we sighted a four-masted bark, in ballast with auxiliary engine, to the N.E. We circled over her a number of times, increasing our radius on each turn until we were nearly out of sight of Ile d'Yeu. We then left the bark and headed for Ile d'Yeu. After searching the shore for mines and submarines, returned to Point Breton.

From Pt Breton we steered course 29 for 45 minutes. We then headed due East for 30 minutes at altitude 50 metres. Motor died and we were forced to make a tail-to-wind landing. We found it possible to land the Tellier in rough water. Dispatched at 2:30 P.M. pigeon with the following message: 'Left Ile d'Yeu at 1:10 P.M., headed 29 for 41 minutes. Then direct East 30 min. had to come down, big sea running. Send all aid.'

Could not tell for certain our location.

We took watches during the night. One bailed while the other two slept. As we could not get motor started, we thought over all possible things that could happen to it. Wilkinson had found that left gas tank had not been feeding; but too late to fix it as we could not see. Passed a very uncertain night. We knew they would do all possible things to help us.

Friday, Nov. 23, 1917

Sent pigeon at 7:40 A.M. and message as follows: 'Sighted last night two lighthouses on starboard bow which we considered Ile d'Yeu. Send torpedo boats and aeroplanes. Have no food. We are taking in water. We are not positive of our location, but are going to sea. Send help. If you do not find us, say we died game to the end.'

Put in new spark plug, cleaned magneto, shifted gasoline from left to right tank. We were all so seasick that we could not work to best advantage. Bailed water out of boat. Wilkinson finally got motor started at 11:40 A.M. Saw hydroplane and blimp to the North of us. Did not give up hope. Beautiful day. Got motor going and started to taxi toward Ile d'Yeu. We were not making much headway on account of the sea. Our left pontoon had filled with water.

Finally decided our only hope was to try and get machine off water. As a result of trying, I broke left wing and got ourselves into a hell of a shape. Things began to look black. There was no finding fault with anyone. Couldn't help marvelling at the morale of the men. It was a case of heroic bravery on their part to see their only hope smashed.

We took part during the night, first lying on wing, then bailing, then sleeping. Wilkinson turned to and got all ready to cast adrift the left wing. We all decided to die game to the end.

Wing began to crumble. We all decided to let it stay on as long as possible. Sea began to grow bitter towards evening, and the water began to come in. We all hoped that we would be able to ride out the night. Very uncomfortable night and we were all growing very weak. Very long night. Our hopes were beginning to go very low, but no one showed it.

Saturday Nov. 24, 1917.

Day finally came. Wing getting near to boat as it crumpled. It was heart-rending. We had to bail and stay out on wing-tip. As waves came over, we began to feel lower and lower. It was finally decided to cast off wing, and let what might come. We tried to get other wing ready to cast off, but we could not get off nuts as we were so weak and tools were inadequate.

We were going over gradually on starboard side. We were all on port side trying to keep her righted. We then saw that there was no way of us staying up much longer unless we could get the wing off. We had just about given up everything when Wilkinson let out a yell that something was in sight. We were not able to believe our eyes. We thought it was a submarine, but we did not care. If it was a submarine, we hoped it would blow us up and end it all.

As luck would have it, the vessel was a French torpedo boat, which pulled alongside

An incident at NAS Le Croisic on 4 March 1918, when the bomb under the port wing fell off and exploded on contact with the water. The explosion almost simultaneously set off the other bomb under the starboard wing, the blast cutting the flying boat in half just behind the cockpit. The rear of the aircraft crashed in pieces back onto the water, while the front section fortunately remained almost intact and slid back onto the water.

the battered wreck of the aircraft and hauled the three crew members aboard to safety. The torpedo boat sank the flying boat with gunfire and took the American sailors back to hospital in La Pallice. Their first taste of wartime action had nearly turned out to be their last, but what it had highlighted was that all aircraft had to be equipped for every emergency, and signalling devices, rations and sea anchors were of paramount importance.

Another incident at NAS Le Croisic on 4 March 1918 was nearly the last for two US Navy aviators, Joe Cline and Frederick Lovejoy. As Cline lifted the flying boat off the water at Le Croisic, the bomb under the port wing fell off and exploded on contact with the water. The explosion almost simultaneously set off the other bomb under the starboard wing, the blast cutting the flying boat in half just behind the cockpit. The rear of the aircraft

crashed in pieces back on to the water, while the front section fortunately remained almost intact and slid back onto the water. Neither man was hurt. Joe Cline was later posted to NAS Brest, where he served with distinction until the Armistice.

The first attack on a German submarine by a US naval aircraft took place on 25 March 1918 when Ensign John F. McNamara, flying from NAS Portland, Dorset, attacked the submarine while it was on the surface. It had disappeared below the surface by the time McNamara had turned for another attack, and he was given a 'probably damaged' evaluation. Later in October, McNamara was posted to NAS Wexford, southern Ireland, where he again attacked a German submarine, this time causing severe damage, but it was still not confirmed as a 'kill'.

Early in February 1918, the US Navy lost its

A Curtiss H.12 on the 'step' about to take off.

first airman in action, Ensign Albert Dillon Sturtevant. He was the epitome of the young eager aviator. He had been educated at Yale University and had joined the Navy to see action. He had finalised his training at RNAS Felixstowe the previous year and had gone on patrol on 15 February at 0900 hours with his co-pilot, Flt Lt Purdy, RNAS, in their Curtiss H.12 together with another H.12 flown by Flt Lt Faux. As they approached the Dutch coast they were attacked by nine German seaplanes, four of which attacked Ensign Sturtevant's aircraft. The following report was sent to Ensign Sturtevant's father when he was told of his son's death:

> On sighting Dutch traffic at 9:55 a.m., 55 miles S. by E. of Felixstowe, machine 4338 and the accompanying 439 were attacked by a formation of nine hostile German seaplanes. Four hostile machines were seen to attack and surround Ens. Sturtevant's machine . . . The last seen of Ens. Sturtevant's machine was 1 and $\frac{1}{2}$ miles to the S.W. of the accompanying machine (4339) . . . From a German report several days later this machine was brought down in flames in the South Downs.

Sturtevant's body and those of his crew were never recovered, and he was awarded the Navy Cross posthumously with the following citation: 'For distinguished and heroic service as an aviator attached to the Royal Air Force Station at Felixstowe, making a great many patrol flights over the North Sea [he] was shot down when engaged gallantly in combat with a number of enemy planes. For the President.'

Aerial shot of USNAS Ile Tudy, France.

On 27 April 1918, one of the Navy's first major successes of the war took place. Ensign Kenneth Smith and his observer, QM1c C.E. Williams, were on patrol from NAS Ile Tudy, near Brest, with another flying boat flown by Ensign Robert H. Harrell and QM1c(A) H.W. Struder, when they spotted the periscope of a German submarine cruising just below the surface of the sea some distance from an incoming convoy. Calling for back-up from a couple of French torpedo boats, Ensign Smith attacked the submarine with his bombs, scoring a direct hit. The French torpedo boats also opened fire and between them they sank the submarine with all hands. For their part in the operation, the two American aviators were awarded the *Croix de Guerre* with Palm.

The naval air station at Ile Tudy was one of the most active, in terms of wartime action, seaplane bases in the war. In another incident on 5 July 1918 concerning a submarine, Ensign Harold Rowen and QM1c C.J. Bolan were alerted to the possible sighting of a German submarine and were scrambled to investigate. After searching the area for over an hour, they spotted something in the water and unloaded their bombs. A violent explosion erupted from the water and oil was seen to spread over the surface, but no debris. It was deemed as a 'possible', but that was all. Two months later Ensign Edwin Pou attacked and sank two German submarines, for which he was awarded the Navy Cross and *Croix de Guerre*.

Surprisingly, it was during this period that the Argentinian Navy decided to send a

Assembling an H.16 flying boat at USNAS Brest, France. 2 November 1918.

USNAS L'Aber Vrach showing all the aircraft ready for launching.

USNAS Queenstown, Ireland.

number of their officers to the United States for flight training. One of them, Ensign Ceferino M. Pouchan, later to become an admiral, was sent to Le Croisic at the beginning of 1918 for seaplane training. He was the only one of the Argentinians to be sent to an active war zone flying station. After completing his training he was sent to Lake Bolsena for further training, and from there on to Malpensa for training on Caproni bombers. He was to end up as the number two aviator in the Argentinian Navy.

By the middle of 1918, the US Navy had a number of patrol aircraft operating from various French bases around the coast: Le Croisic, Brest, L'Aber Vrach and Paimboeuf. In addition to these they and four seaplane patrol bases and one kite balloon base in southern Ireland, at Queenstown, Wexford, Whiddy Island, Lough Foyle and Berehaven. The station at Berehaven on the southern tip of Ireland was the base for kite balloons, thus enabling the convoys arriving from across the Atlantic to be afforded some degree of protection. With command of NAS Killingholme in their hands, the US Navy, together with their Allies, virtually controlled the area of sea between the North Sea and the Channel Islands. The LTA operations of the First World War were overshadowed by the fighter and bomber exploits, but they played an important part in the patrols over the Atlantic approaches.

The sites for the US naval bases had been chosen by the Admiralty in England, and construction work on these bases was started by T.J. Moran & Co., the British Admiralty contractors. With the arrival of the US Navy and the subsequent handing over of the bases to them, the US Navy then completed the construction. The need for a supply base close to the port of Dublin gave rise to the urgent selection of a site. The one chosen was a dilapidated warehouse with no roof or floor, 100 feet wide and 390 feet long, at 76 Sir John Rogerson's Quay in Dublin. It became known as the United States Naval Aviation Supply Base and stored its first materials there in March 1918.

Queenstown became the first NAS in Ireland and was located close to the village of Aghada. On 14 February 1918 it became the headquarters of Commander F. McCrary, USN, Commander US Naval Air Stations, Ireland, although the naval air station itself was under the command of Lt-Cdr Paul J. Peyton. All aircraft that arrived in Dublin in crates were shipped to Queenstown by road for assembly and testing before delivery to their respective air stations. It was also an ideal training base for air crews, as they would be close enough to the war zone without actually being in it. They could be trained to carry out patrols over the Western Approaches without the risk of being attacked by enemy aircraft.

The construction of the base was a source of concern for the Navy, who employed their own labour force comprising local inhabitants, only to find that the necessary equipment was not available. A large, very old and dilapidated steam shovel was found in an abandoned quarry, and after much bargaining with its owner it was dismantled, loaded on to lorries and transported to the site of the base. After a great deal of repair work it was ready, and managed to complete all its excavation tasks before finally giving up the ghost.

After what must have seemed like an eternity, the base was ready to receive its first aircraft. The first 8 seaplanes arrived at Queenstown harbour aboard the USS *Cuyama* on 27 June 1918. From the ship they were placed aboard 'lighters' (a flat barge used for moving large objects from ships in the harbour to shore) and ferried to NAS Queenstown. It is said that it took longer to ferry the aircraft from the ship to the naval air station than it did to bring them from the United States to Queenstown harbour. A further 10 aircraft arrived on 24 July aboard the USS *Kanawha*, and by the end of the war this number had risen to 38. It was not until the end of August that the first of the seaplanes took to the air to carry out any kind of patrol, and it was another couple of months before the first contact with the enemy was made. During October, over 40 patrols were flown accounting for more than 130 hours' flying time.

As the size of the US naval force grew in Ireland, an additional US naval air station was set up at Ferrybank on the Wexford Harbour and was known as NAS Wexford. Construction work by the British Admiralty had started back in December 1917, and it was formally handed over to the US Navy on 2 May 1918. It was commanded by Lt-Cdr Herbster, USN, and comprised two hangars and a variety of other buildings and amenities. Accommodation, unlike the other US naval bases in Ireland, was quite luxurious. Two mansion houses, Bann Aboo and Ely House, were taken over and renovated, and then, after the enlisted men's quarters had been built, turned into the officers' mess.

From NAS Wexford, patrols covered the southern entrance to the Irish Sea, east of Queenstown and just twelve miles from Tuskar Rock lighthouse. It was the busiest area for shipping traffic, as most of the shipping in and out of the United Kingdom passed through its

waters. Consequently it also became the hunting ground of German submarines, and air patrols had to be extremely vigilant when convoys were due in the area.

At the same time as NAS Wexford was being activated, another naval air station, NAS Lough Foyle, this time on the remote northern tip of Ireland, was being constructed. Its location, although ideally placed for a patrol squadron, caused numerous problems for the construction gangs. All materials had to be shipped by sea up to Londonderry and then by road to the site. It was not until 31 July 1918 that the naval air station was completed and ready for operational use. The purchase of a twenty-four-foot whale boat and two dinghies, so that the crews and supplies could be ferried out to the moored seaplanes, all but completed the inventory for the base. All they wanted now were the seaplanes.

Just prior to the opening of the base, a ship from the United States carrying five seaplanes destined for Lough Foyle actually sailed past to the cheers and waves of the air and ground crews who were waiting for the aircraft to arrive. So remote was the base, the aircraft had

A Curtiss H.16 of the US Naval Air Service entering the water for the first US Navy flight from Ireland.

to be taken to Londonderry and unloaded onto trucks before making the round trip back to NAS Lough Foyle. Later, aircraft destined for Lough Foyle were assembled at NAS Queenstown and flown around the coast to the base, using NAS Wexford as a transient base.

Although the seaplanes based in Ireland never had any success in real terms, their presence caused the German Naval High Command to become extremely wary of them. It is an accepted fact that the waters around these patrol areas became among the safest for Allied shipping and not a safe place for the 'Kaiser's tin fish', as one American war correspondent put it.

The first of the US Navy's aircraft to arrive in France from the United States were Curtiss HS-1 seaplanes with Liberty engines. They were assembled at Brest, then delivered to other American stations along the French coast. At first all the air crews were excited with the prospect of getting into the air and joining in the fight; then it was discovered that when they had built the aircraft, the manufacturers had not taken into consideration all the additional equipment that would be necessary to turn the aircraft into a war machine. By the time bombs, machine-guns, radios, Aldis lamps, fire extinguishers, pigeons and enough fuel for a four-hour patrol were installed, the aircraft could not get off the water. Another six feet had to be added to the wing span, and the aircraft was redesignated the HS-2. Even then, three strands of Salmson cord had to be installed on the right rudder to offset the torque, in order to fly the aircraft normally.

The US Navy had also established a base in Italy, at Porto Corsini, some fifty miles south of Venice on the shores of the Adriatic Sea. It was under the command of (then) Lt Willis B. Haviland, but under the direct control of the Italian Director of Marine Aviation. The site of the base at Porto Corsini was at the V-junction of two canals that opened out into the Adriatic Sea, and had been determined because of its location in relation to the Austrian base of Pola

Lt-Cdr Willis B. Haviland standing by one of his squadron's Italian-built Macchi M-5s, with the flying goat insignia on the fuselage.

on the other side of the Adriatic Sea. The battleships and cruisers of the Austrian High Seas Fleet were anchored at Pola, and it was one of the main bases for the German and Austrian submarines that hunted in the Mediterranean.

The US Navy's arrival at Porto Corsini was recognised by the Austrians by their carrying out an attack on the base, but the enemy was unable to inflict any damage or casualties. Initially it was thought there might be a problem with the language, but fortunately the US Navy had realised this, and with Lt Haviland they had sent Naval Aviator Bosun (T) Giochini Varini. Varini had been born in Venice and had emigrated to San Francisco as a young man. The fact that he spoke both English and Italian fluently, and was fully versed in the

A Macchi M.5 operated by Italian Naval Squadron 252A out of Venice, seen here at NAS Porto Corsini.

USNAS Porto Corsini, Italy, from the air. Note the narrowness of the canal and the Macchi seaplane making its take-off.

USNAS Porto Corsini, Italy showing the slipway.

local customs and ways, made the transition and integration of the 300 American Navy men into the community a relatively easy one.

Initially there were problems encouraging the Italians actually to fight the Austrians; they seemed to be content just to carry out observation flights and drop leaflets. Because the US Navy was directly under the control of the Director of Marine Aviation, at first they had to go along with it, but as time progressed they explored the enemy coastline in greater depth and eventually were able to persuade the director to allow them to carry out bombing raids on the Austrian bases. At first it was decided to

Official complement of the US Naval Air Station Porto Corsini, Italy – December 1918.

Macchi M.5 flying boats on the slipway at NAS Porto Corsini.

operate HS-2Ls and Macchi 5s from the base, but the wing span of the HS-2L was far too wide for the canals and the Macchis were only just manageable with great caution. It was decided to use the M.8 seaplane, whose wing span was just under the width of the canal, but there were problems with the very limited bomb loads that could be carried. Training was carried out on Lake Bolsena on an area, marked off by buoys, which equalled the width of the Porto Corsini

A Macchi M.5 flying boat landing in the narrow canal at NAS Porto Corsini.

An Italian Macchi M.5 seaplane navigating the 70-foot wide channel at NAS Porto Corsini, Italy.

US sailors hauling a Macchi M.5 seaplane out of the canal at NAS Porto Corsini, Italy.

Fregattenleütnant Stephen Wollemann sat on the wing of his Phönix D.I. fighter, after shooting down Ensign Ludlow. This was Wollemann's only victory of the war.

A Macchi M.5 No. 13015, flown by Ensign George Ludlow on 21 August, 1918.

Lt Charles Hammann in front of a Macchi M.8 flying boat at NAS Porto Corsini. Note the flying goat insignia on the fuselage with the word Navy on its side.

canals. Within a few weeks the pilots had mastered the take-offs and landings sufficiently to enable the Macchi 5s to be reintroduced.

One of the first contacts with the enemy was on 21 August 1918 when a flight of bombers and fighters from NAS Porto Corsini en route to attack the Austrian base at Pola on the other side of the Adriatic Sea were attacked by a force of Austrian fighters. During the ensuing fight one of the American aircraft was forced down just three miles from the entrance to the harbour at Pola. The pilot, Ensign George Ludlow, managed to get his badly damaged Macchi M.5 seaplane onto the water. Ensign Charles Hammann, even though his own aircraft had been damaged, followed him down and landed alongside Ludlow's now sinking aircraft. Even though he was under constant bombardment from the shore batteries at Pola,

Hammann kept his engine running while Ludlow swam to him. As he clambered onto the floats of Hammann's aircraft, Hammann took off and safely returned to base. For this heroic rescue, Hammann received the Medal of Honor and the Italian Silver Medal of Valour, while Ludlow received the Navy Cross and the Italian Bronze Medal of Valour. (Less than a year later (then) Lieutenant Hammann died in a crash in a Macchi M.5 seaplane.)

The US Navy in Italy actually achieved very little in terms of the war effort in this part of the world, but this was not of their making, more of the Italian High Command's unwillingness to fight. The only American casualty of the air war concerning Porto Corsini was when Ensign Louie J. Bergen crashed while landing his Macchi M.5 on the canal. He died from the resulting injuries.

US naval officers of NAS Porto Corsini. Seated L-R: G.W. Knowles; E.I. Tinkham; C.H. Hammann; J.A. Goggins; J. Stanley. Standing L-R: R.H. Clark; E.L. Smith; C.W. Gates; W. White; A.P. Taliferro; K. Stewart. It is interesting to note the diverse selection of pilot's wings (French and Italian) worn by some of the officers.

At the end of July 1918, the first United States Marine Corps pilots, together with their ground crews and equipment, arrived at Brest, France, en route to their base at Calais. Earlier in the year, Marine Corps Aviator No. 1, Major Arthur Cunningham, had visited France to inspect the French and Italian bomber bases. His primary job was to select bases for the combined Northern Bomber Group pilots who were to follow him from the United States. His main problem, as usual, was that he had more than enough pilots to fill the squadrons, but no aircraft. Cunningham had had earlier problems with the US Army, who had told him quite bluntly that they wanted nothing to do

with him or his pilots: 'If the [marine] squadron ever got to France it would be used to furnish personnel to run one of the [army] training fields, [and] this was as far to the front as it would ever get.'

Cunningham immediately turned to the navy and offered them the services of his Marine Corps pilots in the hunting of and attacking German submarines that operated from the Belgian coast. After consultation with senior navy officers, Cunningham returned to the United States and presented his plan to the General Board of the Navy, stating that his marine pilots could also bomb the German submarine bases, therefore releasing US Navy aircraft to carry out other duties. The Navy Board approved the setting up of a group called the Northern Bombing Group, and Cunningham went down to Miami, Florida, and set about joining up all the other marine units into the 1st Marine Aviation Force.

It was originally planned that the group was to operate as one day wing and one night wing, comprising six squadrons each. The whole group would be under the command of a group commander, the two wings under the command of wing commanders and the six squadrons under the command of squadron commanders. Each of the squadrons was divided into three flights under the command of flight commanders. But on 31 May a cable was received from the Department of the Navy stating that the group be reduced to four day and four night squadrons because of the difficulties of obtaining aircraft.

In America, production of the DH.4 bomber was still only trickling through, so the aircraft Cunningham was offered was the Italian Caproni 600, but he had wanted the Caproni 450 with the Issotta-Fraschini engine. The Caproni 600 had the Italian Fiat engines and had been proved to be most unreliable, and in some cases downright dangerous. Hundreds of the Caproni 600 were ordered by the United States, but only a handful were ever delivered, and the ones that did arrive were plagued with problems of poor-quality workmanship and engine malfunctions. It was said that the Caproni 600 with the Fiat engine killed more Allied crews than the Germans and Austrians combined.

It has also to be remembered that nearly all the American aviators were still in the learning stage of combat, and a large number of them had been assigned to battle-hardened Allied units. As one marine pilot succinctly put it, 'We had flown nothing but Jennies. We got one DH.4, and all of us got one flight in the first DH.4 – one flight! Our gunnery training had consisted of getting into the rear seat and using a Lewis gun, shooting targets on the ground. None of us had ever fired a fixed gun, or

dropped a bomb in our lives.' Nevertheless, these pilots were to become a major asset to the main force of the USAS and US Naval Air Service when they finally arrived, and before the war was over the American pilots and their squadrons would leave their mark on the world of military aviation.

At the beginning of June 1918, a number of US Navy pilots and observers had been assigned to No. 214 Squadron, RAF, at St Inglevert for combat training on Handley Page bombers after their base at Coudekerque had been bombed. By the middle of July the US Navy crews had enough training and experience to go on raids in aircraft manned entirely by American crews. The first of the long-awaited Caproni bombers arrived on 11 August 1918. Four days later the bomber, flown by Ensigns Leslie Taber and Charles Fahy with D.C. Hale as gunner/observer, made a successful night raid on the submarine pens in Ostend. But this was marred by two more missions that had to be aborted because of engine trouble. More time was spent repairing and trying, most of the time unsuccessfully, to keep these aircraft serviceable. The only combat time the American crews were able to get was with No. 214 Squadron on their Handley Page bombers.

After a couple of months of trying to make the Caproni an acceptable bomber, an arrangement was made between the US Army and British authorities to procure British Handley Page bombers in exchange for Liberty engines, to be mounted in the Handley Page aircraft. Unfortunately the agreement was reached and the night bombers tested just as hostilities ceased.

One pilot, Lt (jg) McCormick, USNRF, had carried out a number of these flights at night and was assigned to 214 Squadron RAF to fly bombing missions in the Handley Page. Returning from a bombing mission in the middle of the night, and having suffered flak damage, the aircraft crashed in a forced landing. McCormick managed to extricate himself from the wreckage and then ran forward to aid the RAF members of the crew. In the darkness he ran into one of the large propellers that was still turning and was killed.

On 18 July 1918 the 1st Aviation Force sailed from New York for France aboard the USS *De Kalb*, arriving in Brest on 30 July. It was here that their problems began. There were no arrangements made to move the squadron 400 miles to Calais; in fact no one knew what to do with them. Cunningham requisitioned a train and set about moving his entire force, lock, stock and barrel, to Calais. On arrival, the 1st Aviation Force was billeted temporarily in a British rest camp, before they set to work building their own landing fields. The force had been split into four squadrons: A, B, C and D. A and B Squadrons (commanded by Lts Geiger and McIlvan) were located at a small town by the name of Oye, while C and D Squadrons (commanded by Captain Douglas Roben and 1st Lt Russell A. Presley; D Squadron at the time was still in the United States) were located at La Fresne, just south of Calais. The headquarters for the group was set up in the town of Bois en Andres.

The 1st Marine Aviation Force, as it was now known, was brought up to strength with 149 officers and 842 enlisted men. The original plan of Major Cunningham's of bombing the German submarine pens was shelved because the retreating Germans had evacuated them all. This enabled the marine squadrons, now renumbered 7, 8, 9 and 10, to operate alongside their RAF counterparts in support of the British and Belgian ground forces who were gathering momentum for the final push.

The day wing of the Northern Bombing Group, now under the command of Captain David Hanrahan, USN, was flown by the US Marines, but like their Navy counterparts they were lacking in combat experience. Three crews were assigned to No. 218 Squadron, RAF, for 'hands-on' combat training, and after qualifying returned to their own units. This system proved to be extremely successful, so the American crews were rotated so that at any

one time there was a pool of US Navy and Marine pilots and observers being trained by the RAF.

The US Marine/Navy day-bomber squadrons, however, had more success when they were given DH.4 bombers with Liberty engines. Four of the aircraft were shipped over from the United States and assembled at Pauillac. After being assembled they were inspected by American and British engineers, and after a number of modifications were put into active service. More of the aircraft were expected from the United States, but after a number of delays the Commander US Naval Aviation Forces, Foreign Service, obtained by concession of the British Government fifty-four DH.9 aircraft in exchange for Liberty engines. These aircraft were assembled at Eastleigh and flown across the English Channel to Pauillac, before being assigned to their various squadrons. The first aircraft arrived on 2 October 1918, just too late to make any significant impact on the war.

The marine crews, however, did manage to get involved in operations. Because of a shortage of pilots, the RAF, who had taken a battering over the war years, had more aircraft than crews. An arrangement was made with the two RAF squadrons, Nos. 217 and 218, for the US Marines to fly three bombing missions with them; it was one that gained approval from both sides. On 28 September 1918, while flying with 218 Squadron, RAF, the US Marines scored their first victory when 1st Lt E.S. Brewster and Gunnery Sgt H.B. Wersheiner, although both were wounded when attacked by fighters while over Belgium, shot down a German Albatros. One week later three marine crews, again operating with 218 Squadron, were involved in a dramatic relief operation. The crews – Lt Frank Nelms and Gunnery Sgt Archie Pascal; Captain R.S. Lytle and Gunnery Sgt A. Winman; and Capt. F.P. Mulcahy and Gunnery Sgt T.L. McCullough – dropped over 2,600lb of food and supplies to a beleaguered French regiment who were cut off from the main supply lines. For carrying out

2nd Lt Ralph Talbot, USMC, standing in front of his Curtiss JN4-D.

Gunnery Sgt Robert G. Robinson, USMC.

The crash scene at La Fresne in which 2nd Lt Ralph Talbot, USMC, was killed. This photograph was taken just minutes after the crash.

The wreckage of 2nd Lt Talbot's aircraft at La Fresne.

this dangerous mercy mission the pilots were awarded the Distinguished Service Cross, while the gunnery sergeants were awarded the Navy Cross.

One other raid, carried out on 14 October 1918, concerned eight DH.4s on a bombing mission to carry out a raid on the German-held railway yards at Thielt, Belgium. On the way back from the raid, which was not very successful, the formation was jumped by twelve German fighters. One of the bombers was separated from the others and singled out for attack. The gunner, Gunnery Sergeant Robert G. Robinson, managed to shoot down one of the attackers before he himself was hit. Despite his wounds Robinson continued to fight whilst his pilot, 2nd Lt Ralph Talbot, weaved all over the sky. Robinson was hit twice more and was rendered unconscious. Talbot shot down another of the fighters with his forward-firing fixed guns, then decided that discretion was the better part of valour and put his aircraft into a steep dive. Levelling off at an altitude of 50 feet, Talbot roared over the German lines and landed safely at a Belgium

airfield, where his gunner was taken to hospital for treatment. Robinson recovered and together with Talbot, was awarded America's highest honour – the Medal of Honour. Talbot was killed on 26 October 1918, while carrying out an engine test on an old worn-out DH.4. The engine failed on take-off with the result that the aircraft plunged into an embankment and exploded into flames on contact.

At the end of the war, the US Marine Day Wing in France was credited with shooting down six German aircraft and another eight possibles. The crews were awarded two Medals of Honour, four Distinguished Service Medals and thirty Navy Crosses.

On 13 August 1918, American and British squadrons combined to carry out a raid on the German airfield at Varssenaere. The Germans had been carrying out patrols with their Fokkers and bombing raids on Dunkirk with Gotha bombers from the airfield, causing a great deal of damage. The planning of the raid had been masterminded by Lieutenant-Colonel J.A. Cunningham of the RAF and

Major Harold Fowler of the USAAS. One week previously a rehearsal for the raid had been carried out on the British airfield at Audembert, near Calais, watched by Cunningham and Fowler. On the day of the raid all went according to plan, and when all the aircraft had returned safely, the following communiqué was issued by the RAF.

A RAID WAS CARRIED OUT BY NO. 17 AMERICAN SQUADRON ON THE VARSSENAERE AERODROME, IN CONJUNCTION WITH SQUADRONS OF THE 5TH GROUP. AFTER THE FIRST TWO SQUADRONS HAD DROPPED THEIR BOMBS FROM A LOW HEIGHT, MACHINES OF 17 AMERICAN SQUADRON DIVED TO WITHIN 200 FEET OF THE GROUND AND RELEASED THEIR BOMBS, THEN PROCEEDED TO SHOOT AT HANGARS AND HUTS ON THE AERODROME, AND A CHATEAU ON THE N.E. CORNER OF THE AERODROME WAS ALSO ATTACKED WITH MACHINE-GUN FIRE. THE FOLLOWING DAMAGE WAS OBSERVED TO BE CAUSED BY THIS COMBINED OPERATION: A DUMP OF PETROL AND OIL WAS SET ON FIRE, WHICH APPEARED TO SET FIRE TO AN AMMUNITION DUMP; SIX FOKKER BIPLANES WERE SET ON FIRE ON THE GROUND, AND TWO DESTROYED BY DIRECT HITS FROM BOMBS; ONE LARGE GOTHA HANGAR WAS SET ON FIRE AND ANOTHER HALF DEMOLISHED; A LIVING HUT WAS SET ON FIRE AND SEVERAL HANGARS WERE SEEN TO BE SMOULDERING AS THE RESULT OF PHOSPHORUS BOMBS HAVING FALLEN ON THEM. IN SPITE OF MOST OF THE MACHINES TAKING PART BEING HIT AT ONE TIME OR ANOTHER, ALL RETURNED SAFELY, FAVOURABLE GROUND TARGETS BEING ATTACKED ON THE WAY HOME. NO. 211 SQUADRON BOMBED THE AERODROME AFTER THE LOW-FLYING ATTACK WAS OVER, AND DEMOLISHED THE CHATEAU PREVIOUSLY REFERRED TO.

In France, the German Army had driven a wedge through the French lines at Château-Thierry and a First Brigade was created under the control of General Mitchell in an attempt to support the Army. The American 1st Pursuit Group and 1st Observation Squadron, together with some French squadrons, made up the First Brigade and were soon in action against the Germans. It was to become a 'baptism under fire' for nearly all the American pilots, as they came up against a hardcore of experienced German pilots whose machines were far superior to theirs. In the weeks that followed before the German push was halted, American pilots became hard-bitten and experienced and aged about five years in as many weeks. They suffered terrible losses both in the air and on the ground, but the tide had turned.

But not all the American pilots were the epitome of the 'All-American Boy'. There were among them a few mavericks, and none more so than 2nd Lieutenant Frank Luke from Arizona, a member of No. 27 Pursuit Squadron. Luke's family background was pure German. His father was born in Prussia and his mother was descended from the first German settlers on Long Island, but that is where the connection ended. The Luke family was as patriotic as any natural-born Americans.

Frank Luke's career started at Rockwell Field Flying School, San Diego, where he passed the course without difficulty and obtained his wings. In July 1918 he was posted to France and assigned to the 27th Pursuit Squadron, under the command of a Canadian, Major Harold E. Hartney, RCFC. It was soon discovered that despite his ancestry, 2nd Lt Frank Luke had not inherited the German trait of discipline. Major Hartney was a much-respected commander. A former volunteer in the Saskatchewan Fusiliers, he had transferred to the RFC and served with No. 20 Squadron RFC during the period of 'Bloody April' in 1917. A highly experienced combat pilot, he slowly got through to Frank Luke that the day of the 'lone gunfighter' was over, and survival now depended on teamwork.

On the other hand there were the 'All-American Boys' who fought in the war and adhered strictly to the rules, and none more so

Lt Frank Luke with members of his ground crew.

than Captain Eddie Rickenbacker, who was the complete opposite of Frank Luke. Rickenbacker was to become America's top ace with a score of twenty-six, the vast majority of these shot down in a two-month period. He had come into flying late in life, having been a sergeant driver for General Pershing for a period of time. His background as a racing driver was to help him master the complexities of flying an aircraft. He was not a natural pilot, but one who had to work at all the problems that flying in combat brought with it.

Rickenbacker soon tired of being General Pershing's chauffeur and looked around for a position that would move him closer to the world of aviation. Then, by luck he met General Billy Mitchell, whose 'official' car was a fast sports car and who wanted nothing better than a noted racing driver as his chauffeur. Despite his lack of college education he persuaded General Mitchell to put him forward for pilot training and was assigned to an aviation unit. On completion of an engineering course, he was given a commission and assigned to Issoudon initially as the engineering officer. Frustrated with his position and the length of time it was taking to be accepted into flying training, he managed to persuade the instructors to give him some lessons in their spare time. After some weeks his orders to flight school came through, and after only five-and-a-half hours of dual control flying, he went

Major Harold E. Hartney.

solo. His experience as a racing driver stood him in good stead, as did his skill as a mechanic.

He was posted to Issoudon, the base for replacement aircraft where all the major repair work was done. Rickenbacker's job was to test the aircraft after they had been repaired, a job which again soon bored him. He was then posted to the aerial gunnery school at Cazeaux where, after two weeks of intense practice, he passed out with flying colours. Then followed a posting on 3 March 1918 to a new squadron, No. 94 Pursuit Squadron at Villeneuve under the command of Major Jean Huffer. It was to be a month before their aircraft arrived, and Rickenbacker made his first flight over the lines with Major Raoul Lufbery (Lufbery was killed the following month).

It did not take him long to realise that flying training was one thing, but flying in combat was something totally different. Rickenbacker was not a natural pilot, so everything he did had to be thought out prior to doing it. Combat, he realised, was going to comprise loops, rolls and tight turns, all done in a split second, because that could mean the difference between life and death. He developed his own training programme of various manoeuvres and soon became adept at them. The slow build-up for his squadron to become fully operational was to his advantage, and when the first of the action arrived he was somewhere near ready.

On 29 April, six weeks after arriving at the squadron, Rickenbacker scored his first victory – a Pfalz. He had been flying with James Hall over Pont-à-Mousson when they encountered the German aircraft on a reconnaissance mission. After the experienced Hall had climbed into the sun and attacked, forcing the German aircraft to turn into Rickenbacker's path, Rickenbacker shot the Pfalz fighter down in flames. The following month the intrepid pair were flying patrol when they encountered a patrol of German aircraft. Rickenbacker shot down his second, an Albatros D.III, but Hall's aircraft was hit, by what fortunately later turned out to be a dud shell. Fighting the controls of the badly damaged aircraft, Hall managed to crash-land just inside the German lines. The aircraft hit the ground with such force that Hall's face was smashed violently into the butts of his guns. Badly injured, he was extricated from the wreckage by his German captors and taken to a field hospital. There he was treated by doctors, but his war was over.

One month later Rickenbacker chalked up his fifth 'kill', and with it came promotion to flight commander, although he retained his rank of captain and was not given the rank of major which usually went with the position. Maybe it was his background and lack of college education that was holding him back, because it has to be remembered that it was not only the RFC who nurtured class distinction. But Rickenbacker was admired by his fellow pilots because he would not ask them to do anything that he would not do. He stressed teamwork all the time to both the ground crews and the pilots. His knowledge of engines surpassed even the best of flight mechanics, and he was not averse to getting his hands dirty when the need arose. He communicated with everyone all the time, developing a team spirit second to none. He was not a 'death and glory' pilot either, but one who was methodical and assessed situations before embarking upon them. This is not to say that he would shy away from a fight; on the contrary, he could scrap with the best of them. But he was mature enough to know that discretion was the better part of valour. It was this attitude that was to lead him to become America's top fighter ace with the 94th Pursuit Squadron and be awarded his country's highest accolade, the Medal of Honor, albeit some eight years after the war had ended.

Chapter 6

September – November 1918:
The Final Push

The 2nd Pursuit Group, which comprised the 13th, 22nd, 49th and 139th Pursuit Squadrons, operated out of the Toul area. When the squadrons first arrived, the majority of the pilots were fresh from training, but the 139th Squadron, commanded by Major Angstrom, that had spearheaded the group was joined by three of the USAS's most experienced pilots: Captain David Putnam from the Lafayette Flying Corps, and Captains Ray Bridgman and Dudley Hill from the *Escadrille Lafayette*.

But it was not the quality of the pilots that concerned the Americans, but the lack of aircraft. Fortunately, the French aircraft manufacturers had been stirred into increasing their production of SPADs, Breguets and Salmson 2-A2s. Unfortunately, the pilots and mechanics had all been trained on rotary-engined aircraft and not the watercooled ones like the Hispano-Suiza V-8s. Not only did the water-cooled-engined aircraft have their own flying idiosyncrasies, but tuning the aircraft engines with virtually no spares also caused its own problems. A complete retraining programme had to be thought out, and this in the middle of the final push of the war. The commanding officer, Major Angstrom, decided that as far as the mechanics were concerned it would be quicker to send the best of his mechanics to the French Air Service acceptance park at Etampes and have them follow a crash course in maintenance on the new types of aircraft. After numerous problems, the main one being the language barrier, the mechanics returned to Vaucouleurs and immediately spread themselves around to give instruction to the remainder of the ground crews. The engineering officer used the handbooks extensively, and in doing so realised that the Hispano-Suiza engine, although an excellent engine, had to be handled with meticulous care and tuned like a racing engine.

The pilots, on the other hand, trained themselves through a system of trial and error. Fortunately for all concerned, the American sector at that time was quiet, but it was to be the quiet before the storm. On 11 September came Battle Order No. 1 from General Mitchell: 'Our Air Service will take the offensive at all points, with the objective of destroying the enemy's air service, attacking his troops on the ground, and protecting our own air and ground troops.' Lt-Col Atkinson, who had been recently promoted from major, issued his order from the Headquarters of the 1st Pursuit Squadron on the same day: 'The entire 3rd Pursuit Group will be on alert after 0900 hrs, subject to the call of the Chief of Air Service. It will be prepared to carry out missions of bombardment and to attack designated objectives on the ground.' Captain Robert Rockwell, who only days earlier had replaced Major Thaw as commander of the 103rd Pursuit Squadron, also issued an order, in the name of Major Thaw: 'All available planes, including those with bomb racks installed, will be held on alert from eight o'clock, ready to leave within ten minutes after receiving a call from this office.'

The new tactics of low-level strafing were completely new to the majority of the pilots of the 3rd Pursuit Group, and left the aircraft extremely vulnerable to ground fire. But the big push by the American infantry at St Mihiel needed all the support it could get, and General Mitchell was determined not to be found wanting when the time came. All the SPADs of 103rd Squadron were equipped with bomb racks capable of taking twenty-pound bombs. Their round-trip would take them on the route Vaucouleurs–Mars la Tour–Chambley–Arnaville–Chambley–Vaucouleurs at heights that ranged from ground level to 500 feet.

On the evening of 11 September 1918, Colonel Davenport Johnson called his squadron leaders to a briefing – the St Mihiel offensive would start at 0500 hours the following morning. Captain David Putnam, who was standing in for his commanding officer Major Angstrom, looked at the wet, misty weather and wondered what part they would be able to play in the forthcoming battle. By dawn the whole camp was alive with anticipation, and as daylight broke through the driving mist, the mechanics wheeled the aircraft out and started the engines. After ten minutes the engines were shut down and the vital parts of the aircraft covered with tarpaulins against the increasingly inclement weather. Colonel Johnson issued an order: 'Pilots and ground crews will mess in rotation by flights until further notice. Return to alert positions as soon as possible.'

Throughout the morning the squadron commanders waded backwards and forwards in the ever-thickening mud, between the hangars and the offices. It was to be lunchtime before the first of the aircraft were ordered to fly a patrol. The airfield by this time resembled a muddy, ploughed field, and the inevitable accident occurred. Lieutenant Joe Carr of the 139th Pursuit Squadron was taxiing to take-off when his propeller hit a large clump of mud and disintegrated. His ground crew spent the rest of the morning manhandling his aircraft through the mud on a tail dolly back to its hangar for repair. Finally, six of the pilots managed to get their aircraft into the air, but in less than an hour they were on their way back – or at least some of them were. The pilots had not seen anything of the enemy; indeed, they had seen very little at all and had had great difficulty in finding their way back. Two of them had to force-land due to engine problems and mechanics had to be sent to repair the aircraft.

By mid-afternoon the weather had eased enough for a two-man patrol to be sent out. Led by Captain David Putnam and accompanied by Lieutenant Wendell Robertson, the patrol set off for a reconnaissance of the front lines. They met up with an enemy patrol, and in the ensuing mêlée they were separated. Robertson returned to the airfield alone, and the following morning Putnam's body was found in the wreckage of his aircraft inside the American lines.

In the Toul sector, No. 1 Observation Squadron was carrying out reconnaissance flights over the enemy lines. They were joined by the 96th Bombardment Squadron (Red Devils), who were to be the first day bombardment squadron to see action, flying French Breguet 14Bs. The creation of the 1st Day Bombardment Group on 10 September 1918, under the command of Major James Dunsworth, had also meant the addition of two more bomber squadrons, the 11th and 20th. These two squadrons were armed with American-built DH.4s, but when they tried to replace the ageing Breguet 14Bs of the 96th, the move was strongly resisted. The pilots and ground crews had mastered all the idiosyncrasies of the French aircraft and could see no

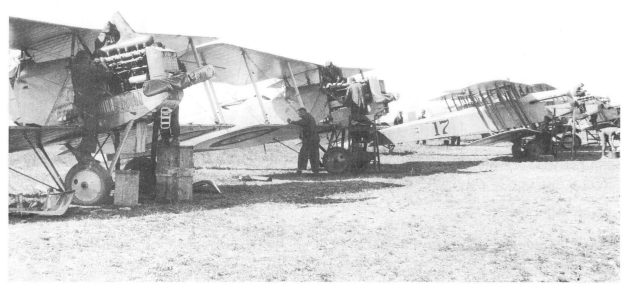

Breguet 14-B2 of the 89th Squadron, USAS, being worked on and maintained at Chatillon-sur-Seine in June 1918.

Major Thomas Bowen; Lt George and Lt Howard G. Rath of the 1st Day Bombardment Group.

Members of the 20th Bombardment Squadron. L-R: Lts Stokes; Holt; Howard; Captain Sellers; Lts Willis; Koepfgen; Fiske and Schultz.

point in learning about a new aircraft at this late stage of the war.

The 11th and 20th Bombardment Squadrons were sent to Colombey-les-Belles to collect their DH.4s, only to find that the aircraft had been parked, exposed to the elements without cover for a number of weeks. The ground crews set-to immediately to dry out the aircraft, re-tension the flying wires, and check the rigging and engines to bring them up to operational standard. On 10 September orders came from Group Headquarters to convert all the 11th and 20th Squadron aircraft to bombers and prepare them for the St Mihiel offensive. The problem was that the squadrons had neither bombs nor bomb racks, but by the next morning, after numerous heated telephone calls, all the equipment arrived, and by midday on 11 September twelve DH.4s with

tarpaulins over the engines and cockpits were fuelled, bombed and armed, ready to go.

At one minute past midnight on 12 September 1918, the St Mihiel offensive began with a barrage from 3,000 guns that was to be constant until dawn, when the 550,000 American and 110,000 French troops on the ground would make their push forward. But in the air, the weather had closed in and all aircraft were grounded. The previous night, all along the Front, US and French balloon companies had been preparing their observation balloons for the assault. Ten miles to the north of St Mihiel, the 2nd Balloon Company, one of fourteen balloon companies in the US Army, had spent most of the night preparing its balloon, and as dawn broke, so did the weather. With winds that gusted up to 50 mph, and while the men on the ground payed out the

Lt Guy Weiser of the 20th Bombardment Squadron, visiting Transchultz Castle, Landshut, Bavaria where he was a POW in 1918 after being shot down.

cable, the observers in the basket held on for dear life. At 400 feet the observers peered through the driving rain as the basket, hanging precariously below the inflated gas bag, rocked violently backwards and forwards, and watched as American infantrymen moved forwards. The going at first was relatively slow because of the adverse weather conditions, but as the morning progressed it gained momentum. By noon the positions of the balloon companies had to be reassessed as they could no longer see the front line of troops.

By midday the weather had cleared enough for nine of the DH.4s from the 96th Bombardment Squadron to take off to bomb Bruxières. By mid-afternoon seven of the nine aircraft had returned, two having been shot down by an enemy patrol that jumped the bombers while on their way back. Another

eight Breguets left later in the afternoon, again to bomb Bruxières – all returned safely. Later the same afternoon another raid on Bruxières resulted in three aircraft crashing in the darkness on their return. At the end of the day the 96th Bombardment Squadron had lost three pilots and eight aircraft and had a number of other aircraft with minor damage.

Among the other casualties on the first raids was 1st Lieutenant Codman of the 96th Bombardment Squadron, who, together with his observer, was shot down. His report describing the incident and capture of both men, culminating in the escape of Lt Codman, can be found in Appendix 1. The 96th Bombardment Squadron was carrying out a bombing raid on Conflans during the St Mihiel offensive at the time of Lt Codman's incident, when he and three other crews flying

Men of the 2nd Balloon Company, USAS, at Montreuil, France on 8 July 1918, firing on enemy aircraft that were attacking their balloon.

Breguet No. 18 of the 96th Bombardment Squadron with Lt Alexander (pilot) and Lt John McLennan (bombardier/gunner) aboard.

Breguet bombers were attacked. Because of their inexperience they had broken the cardinal rule of all bombing squadrons: never fly without fighter cover if the squadron is flying well below operational strength. All four of the bombers were shot down, and only Lt Codman and his observer, Lt Stewart A. McDowell, survived. The squadron may well in this case have thought that because it was only a relatively short flight to Conflans they could do without the cover, but it was an expensive lesson to learn and it was not the first time it was to happen, and most certainly not the last.

On the morning the offensive began, the 103rd began opportunity bombing of the trenches and roads. The 1st and 3rd Pursuit Groups caught a heavy concentration of enemy troops on the road between Creuse and Vigneulles later in the morning and attacked them with machine-gun fire and bombs, causing considerable damage and confusion. The 1st Day Bombardment Group also carried out a number of very successful missions on the first day of the offensive, despite the ferocious anti-aircraft fire (archie), and dropped in excess of 13,120 kg of bombs on railroads, troop concentrations and dumps. Although the rewards were high, so was the price. The first week of the St Mihiel offensive cost the 1st Bombardment Group dearly: they lost thirty-five officers and men during raids over the lines.

By 15 September the offensive had pushed the Germans back significantly and the tide had turned. The line was firmly established from Haudimont, through Frenes-en-Woevre, Doncourt and Jaulny to Vandières, north of Pont-à-Mousson. But after the initial surge the drive forward was slowing noticeably, due to three German observation balloons that were spotting for the artillery with unerring accuracy. Major Hartney of the 27th Pursuit Squadron called Lt Frank Luke into his office and explained the problem. Together with Lt Joe Wehner, Frank Luke took off at 6.45 p.m. and sped towards where the balloons were

thought to be. At 7.10 the sky in the north-east beyond Verdun suddenly flared red; eleven minutes later the sky flared red again; and fifteen minutes after that the last of the balloons flared red against the black sky. Hartney had flares lit on the airfield for the returning pilots, delighted that they had accomplished what was at first thought would be a suicidal and almost impossible mission. With the balloons down, the rumble of trucks and the sound of soldiers' boots pounding on the roads increased, and the drive forward carried on in earnest. The following are the respective incident reports of Frank Luke and Joe Wehner:

Patrolled to observe enemy activity. Left a little after the formation, expecting to find it on the lines. On arriving there I could not find formation, but saw artillery firing on both sides; also saw light at about 500 meters. At first I thought it was an observation machine, but on nearing it I saw that it was a Hun balloon, so I attacked and destroyed it. I was archied with white fire and machine guns were very active. Returned very low. Saw thousands of lights in woods north of Verdun. On account of darkness coming on I lost my way and landed in a wheat field at Agers at about 21h30. Balloon went down in flames at 19h50. A true copy.

Left airdrome after formation expecting to pick them up at the Front. I was instructed to attack enemy balloons with Lt Luke, so I stayed at a low altitude. Saw formation coming north so flew towards the Hun lines to pick up a balloon. Attacked a balloon N.E. of Verdun and S.W. of Spincourt at about 17h10 bringing it down. I was forced to pull off immediately as a formation of five Hun planes were trying to cut me off, and my guns were empty. Hun planes were both Fokker and Albatross [sic]. I manoeuvred down towards

Lt Fritz Wehner, USAS, wingman of Lt Frank Luke.

during this incident, while Frank Luke escaped by the skin of his teeth. From that moment on Luke's hatred for the Germans filled his mind to the exclusion of everything else, a potentially dangerous frame of mind for a combat pilot to be in, and one that was to eventually be his downfall.

When Major Hartney was promoted to group commander, Captain Alfred Grant took over. Frank Luke and Alfred Grant took an instant dislike to each other, with the result that Luke lapsed into his old ways of indiscipline. Grant was a military martinet and demanded discipline, something that had always eluded Frank Luke. Despite their animosity towards each other, Grant could not help but have a grudging respect for the skill and bravery of Frank Luke. Luke had already shot down a number of German aircraft, and shown a propensity for attacking and destroying enemy observation balloons.

On 26 September 1918, Frank Luke and his new chosen wingman, Lt Ivan Roberts from Massachusetts, took off to attack a German observation balloon operating between Consenvoye and Sivry. Frank Luke's report of the mission described the incident from which only he returned:

Chambley where the Huns left me, after seeing a formation of French SPADs approaching. I fired approximately 100 rounds into the balloon.

The potentially dangerous game of 'balloon-busting' was one that had attracted Frank Luke and his close friend Joseph Wehner (also from a German family and, because of his name, constantly subjected to the unfounded suspicions of over-zealous intelligence officers), and together they became one of the best 'balloon-busting' teams in the USAS. They would watch each other's tails while one or the other attacked a balloon. That was until one mission, when Frank Luke attacked two balloons while his friend fought off six enemy fighters. Wehner was shot down and killed

On patrol to strafe balloons in vicinity of Consenvoye and Sivry, I attacked with two others a formation of five Fokkers. After firing several short bursts, observed the Hun go down out of control. While at 100 meters I was attacked by two e.a., so I did not see the first e.a. crash. I turned on the other two who were on my tail, getting on the tail of one . . . One confirmation requested. The last I saw of Lt Roberts, who was on this patrol with me, was in combat with several Fokkers in the vicinity of Consenvoye and Sivry.

No trace was ever found of Lt Ivan Roberts or his aircraft, and one can only assume that he crashed and was burnt out of all recognition.

Frank Luke claimed another balloon on the 27th when, observed by Lt Joseph N. Fox, he attacked a balloon near Marieulles. He made three passes at the balloon as it was being winched down, and it was on the third pass when the balloon was near the ground that it burst into flames, falling on top of the winch and the German crew. Luke tried to land in a field nearby to confirm the 'kill', but his engine was giving him trouble so he returned to his field and rode back to the site on his motorcycle.

In a meteoric career that lasted no more than a few months at the Front, Frank Luke was awarded the Medal of Honor (the first to be awarded to the USAS) and a Distinguished Service Cross, but never lived long enough to wear either. His flying career consisted of only thirty hours of combat flying, but during this brief moment in time he downed nineteen enemy aircraft and fifteen observation balloons, becoming the second-highest ace in the USAS. His death came after he had taken off on an unauthorised flight and attacked and destroyed three balloons, but was badly wounded during the last of the attacks. He managed to crash-land his aircraft near the village of Murvaux five miles east of Dun-sur-Meuse, but not before he had shot up the main street full of Germans. Badly wounded, he dragged himself towards a stream nearby. The German soldiers called for him to surrender; his reply was to open fire with his Colt .45 pistol, but then he collapsed with a bullet through his lungs.

It was later ascertained that he had received the fatal wound while making his strafing run and died as he had lived, a 'lone gunfighter'. His body was stripped of all identification by the Germans, thrown on to a handcart and taken to the local graveyard, where it was left to the French villagers to bury. He was later identified by a wristwatch that had been overlooked by the Germans. After the war *Leutnant* Mangels, who had commanded one of the balloon companies attacked by Frank Luke on that day, said that he had gone to Murvaux after being told that the American who had shot down two of his balloons had himself been shot down. He saw Frank Luke's body in the churchyard and confirmed everything that the French villagers had said about the incident.

In his recommendation for Frank Luke's Medal of Honor, Lt-Col O.C. Aleshire wrote:

> On Sept. 29th, 1918, Lieut. Luke, after having dropped from his plane a note to the 7th U.S. Balloon Company reading 'Watch for burning balloons. Luke', attacked and shot down in flames three enemy balloons despite extremely heavy fire from the ground and from a formation of eight enemy planes protecting the balloons. Although mortally wounded in this combat, and although more than ten kilometers within enemy territory, Lieut. Luke descended to within fifty meters of the town of Murvaux and opened fire with his machine guns, killing six enemy soldiers and wounding many more. He then landed, stood by his plane, and when surrounded and called upon to surrender, drew his automatic and held off the enemy until he died from the effects of his wound.

Lt Frank Luke broke virtually every rule in the book, objected to military discipline, and, had he returned from his last flight, would undoubtedly have been charged for going absent without leave and court-martialled for actually going on the flight without permission. The 'Balloon Buster from Arizona' was just twenty years old at the time of his death.

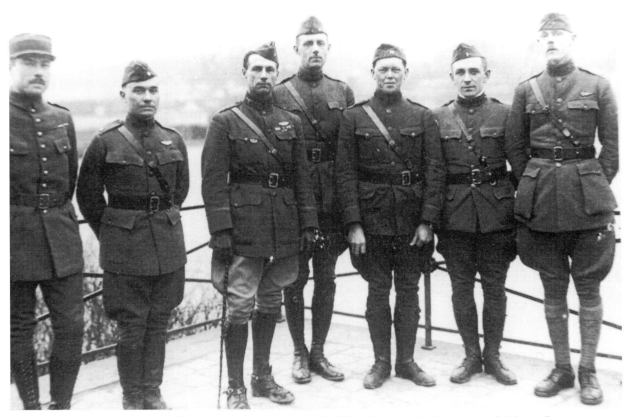

General Mitchell with members of his staff in Paris. L-R: Capt. R. Vallois (French Air Service); Lt-Col Lewis Brereton; General Mitchell; Major I.S. Joralemon; Capt. O.F. Marvel; Lt E.F. Schwab; Lt Paul Mathis.

The continuing bad weather was making General Mitchell – not famed for his patience – extremely irritable, as he had hoped to prove that his air force was a necessary part of the offensive in supporting the ground troops. He had visions for the future and wanted the world to see what a properly equipped and trained air force could contribute to a military situation. Of the sixteen squadrons General Mitchell had at his disposal, only six were at full strength; the remainder for a variety of reasons were well under strength. His aim to let the ground front-line troops see the support they were getting from his airborne squadrons was excellent in theory, but in reality a non-starter. The main problems were that the bombers would be attacking targets well beyond their own lines, and the escort fighters

accompanying them would be flying at medium to high altitudes. Consequently, the only aircraft that the front-line troops would see would be the reconnaissance ones. Added to this was the fact that the majority of the troops could not identify one aircraft from another in any case, so they would have no idea of the nationality or type of any of the aircraft.

On the second day of the St Mihiel offensive, with the threat of the German observation balloons now removed, the weather eased and patrols were increased. The US and French balloon companies moved forward and consolidated new positions. Contact with the enemy was still sparse, but over the next couple of days the Germans lost a few more of their aircraft. In the meantime the Front had moved away from Toul, and on 24 September 1918 it was decided that the 2nd Pursuit Group should be moved to Belrain, about eight miles west of Verdun. The move also prompted a change of tactics. Bomb racks were fitted to the SPADs, the ground staff labouring through the night of 25/26 September to ensure all the aircraft were ready for the low-level ground strafing and bombing that the aircraft were about to be subjected to.

Ground strafing was one of the most dangerous aspects of military warfare. Flown usually at heights between 50 and 200 feet, the object was to attack columns of ground troops, their artillery, horses, vehicles and troop and supply trains, inflicting the heaviest of casualties possible on both men and equipment. The first passes by the aircraft were often the safest, due in the main to the element of surprise; by the time the aircraft made its second pass, the ground troops would have recovered from the surprise attack and would sometimes reply with devastating ground fire. Many an aircraft returned with the fabric covering the wings and fuselage in tatters.

The weather in the area continued to cause problems for the squadrons. Strong, gusty winds accompanied by rain hampered the observation and attack aircraft, especially those flown by pilots on their first missions. Yet despite this the squadrons continued to take their toll on the enemy and the offensive petered out in favour of the Allies. On the ground, the maintenance crews were performing nothing short of miracles. Changing and repairing engines, replacing propellers and patching up tattered airframe fabric, some of which looked like patchwork quilts, were all carried out under the most appalling conditions.

With the German Army still reeling from the offensive, the order came for a concerted attack by the Allies on the Front between the Meuse and the Suippe Rivers. The place for the attack, the Meuse River and Argonne Forest area, had been General Pershing's choice. The First Corps was to attack on the front between Verignois and La Harazée, with the 35th, 28th and 77th Divisions in line from left to right. Attached to the 28th Division was the 12th Observation Squadron for all required aviation duties. The 12th had been chosen for this duty as it was now one of the most experienced of all the American squadrons, and this was hopefully to be the last major battle of the war. Orders from General Mitchell were that all flights over the Meuse–Argonne area were to be made in French aircraft, so as not to make the Germans aware of the huge build-up of American troops. He ordered that the 1st Day Bombing Group carry out raids on the city of Metz and its surrounding railway yards, so as to make the enemy think that the point of any offensive by the Allies might be there.

The group suffered heavy casualties in terms of men and machines during this period. All American aircraft to be used in the offensive were brought into position over the preceding days, so that on the afternoon of the 25th they were all in position and ready, while the balloon regiments near the Front itself remained inactive until late in the afternoon of the 25th, when they started to inflate their balloons. Mitchell then quietly moved his headquarters to Souilly, so as to be close to the Front when the offensive began.

The reason for the secrecy was because the day before, 24 September, a German reconnaissance aircraft had been shot down and undamaged photographic plates were found in the wreckage. When developed, they showed General Pershing's headquarters and a very large area surrounding it, highlighting the build-up of troops and their weapons. Whether or not the Germans had wind of something Pershing was not sure, but one thing was certain: a complete security cordon had to be thrown around the whole area.

The Meuse–Argonne offensive, as it was to become known, started just after midnight on 26 September 1918, when 2,700 Allied guns, just behind the infantry's jump-off point, opened up on the enemy's positions. After five hours of continuous bombardment 600,000

Souilly airfield, home of the 88th, 99th and 104th Observation Squadrons during the St Mihiel offensive.

men, predominantly Americans, went over the top and into the final major battle of the war. The weather could not have been worse: torrential rain, thick mist and acres of mud. The intention was to drive wedges through the Hindenburg Line for about the first 16 kilometres, then to go for a second push for a further 16 kilometres with the Americans heading for Sedan to capture the major railway centre there, thus preventing any reserves from being brought up. The British were to attack from the Western Front and the French to push through the Champagne area.

The balloon companies raised their observation balloons all along the Front, attracting Fokker D.VIIs like moths to a flame. The 8th Balloon Company raised and lowered their balloon time and time again as it was attacked, then late in the afternoon of the 26th, at a height of 1,200 metres, it was attacked again, only this time it was set on fire. The two observers in the basket, Lts C.J. Ross and H.E.

Hudnut, jumped for their lives. Hudnut jumped first, his parachute opening very soon after leaving the basket; Ross, on the other hand, waited until Hudnut was clear before he too jumped. Unfortunately, burning remnants of the balloon fell upon his parachute as it deployed and collapsed it. Ross plunged to the ground and was killed, the first balloon observer to be killed in the action. That particular Fokker D.VII accounted for a further three American balloons that afternoon.

The 9th Balloon Company lost its first balloon on 28 August 1918, when a Fokker D.VII appeared from nowhere and riddled the canopy with machine-gun fire. Fortunately Lt Sheldon Clarke and Cpl Lionel Bailey managed to jump to safety and were able to watch with some satisfaction as their own machine-gunners brought the enemy aircraft down. On 12 September they raised their second balloon, only to see it destroyed by enemy artillery fire. Ten days later the incident was repeated, only

Men of the 8th Balloon Company operating a winch to control the ascent of their balloon.

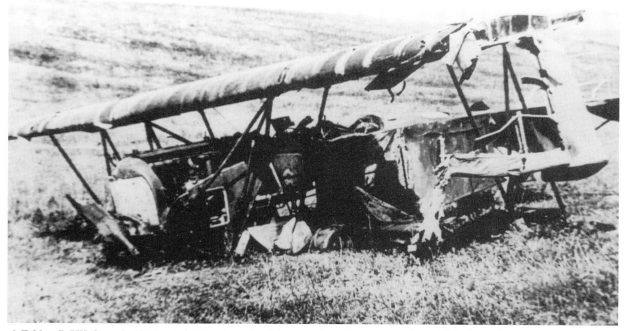

A Fokker D.VII flown by Feldwebel *Marwitz, after being shot down by gunners of the 9th Balloon Company during an attack on their balloon.*

Sopwith F1 Camel of the 185th Squadron, USAS with a 160hp Gnôme Monosoupape engine and a 37mm cannon through the propeller shaft.

this time they were in the process of inflating the balloon when it was hit. In the following weeks, as they were to follow the advancing troops, they were to lose two more balloons, but the war was over before there were any more casualties.

The initial advance was slowed significantly as it approached the Meuse River. The Germans still held the high ground above the Meuse River and the Bois d'Appremont and were able to get six divisions into the area. No-man's-land was a quagmire, and it took General Pershing five days to get his heavy artillery into position to pound the German positions. On 7 October 1918, the American Army launched a major assault on the German positions and gradually clawed their way onto the high ground and secured it. As the exhausted German Army fell back their resis-

tance crumbled and soon they were in full retreat. The initial early successes gave rise to speculation that it was to be a short-lived offensive in favour of the Allies, and that all resistance would soon peter out. This was to prove very wrong indeed, and the Germans counter-attacked on 8 October 1918. To protect their troops, the German High Command marshalled more and more aircraft into the sector as the American 1st Army counter-attacked almost immediately. The result was that aerial fighting became a daily occurrence, and within weeks novice pilots either became battle-hardened or just did not survive.

It was decided by the USAS High Command that a night-fighter squadron might be of help to keep the pressure on the enemy and the momentum of the advance going. A collection of SPADs were put together with pilots who were between squadrons, and placed under the command of Captain Seth Low. The squadron became known as the 185th Night Pursuit Squadron and became operational on 18 October 1918. No sooner had the SPAD aircraft been allocated to the 185th than it was decided that they were required as replacements for other squadron aircraft. Seth Low finally got the squadron up to the front at Erize-la-Petite, but with no aircraft. Five days later fourteen Sopwith Camels arrived powered by Gnôme Monosoupape engines – the squadron was in business.

It was not the success that was hoped. None of the pilots had done any night flying, the aircraft had no night-flying instruments and there were no landing lights on the aircraft or on the airfields. Casualties started to pile up, and when Seth Low was replaced by Captain Jerry Vasconcells, the night-flying programme was unofficially put on hold and then slowly allowed to fade into obscurity.

The counter-attack on the ground soon fizzled out, but the battle in the air was still being fought, and it was to rage on right up until 1100 hours on 11 November 1918, when Germany capitulated and the Armistice was signed. The following week of the Meuse–Argonne offensive saw the USAS carrying out raids on the retreating German Army and their lines of communication, but at a cost of over twenty aircraft and thirty-six experienced air crew. The commanders were struggling desperately to keep up the morale of their respective squadrons, but the American airmen were having a hard time coming to terms with the sudden loss of their friends. The 50th Observation Squadron, who were attached to the 77th Infantry Division, prior to carrying out reconnaissance missions over their area painted a large insignia of the Statue of Liberty on the sides of their aircraft. The squadron pilots and observers felt this was necessary because of previous problems with infantry divisions, which had fired upon their aircraft due to poor, or in some cases, non-existent aircraft recognition instruction.

Lt Daniel Morse, Commanding Officer of the 50th Observation Squadron, experienced great difficulty liaising with the 77th Infantry Division. On 2 October, after twelve hours of flying through rain, fog and the dense smoke drifting up from the battlefields below, the squadron had achieved virtually nothing. Meanwhile, on the ground, the 77th Infantry Division had been pushing on into the Argonne Forest, oblivious to the fact that they had lost nearly all contact with the 50th Observation Squadron. The 2nd Battalion, 308th Infantry Division, commanded by Major Charles Whittlesey, had in fact lost all contact with the Air Service.

The 2nd Battalion was in the process of a combined attack with the French 1st Dismounted Cavalry Division on a hill aptly named *Moulin de L'Homme Mort* (Dead Man's Mill), with the express purpose of pushing the Germans off the surrounding hills and ridges. The Americans made good progress and fought their way past the hill, pushing the Germans back; the French, on the other hand, did not sustain their attack and were halted. They then retreated to regroup and resupply without letting their American counterparts know what was going on. The Americans, oblivious to all this, pushed forward, creating a gap in the offensive line. The Germans, on seeing the gap, pushed their troops forward and behind the American lines, cutting them off. With no contact with their headquarters or the French, the 2nd Battalion was in trouble.

Major Whittlesey and his troops were trapped in a ravine surrounded by Germans, subjected to heavy fire from rifles and mortars. Whittlesey sent their co-ordinates out by carrier-pigeon, but they were woefully wrong and at one point they even found themselves under 'friendly' fire from an American battery. The battalion found themselves short of food and ammunition after days of continuous combat and were reduced to looking for rations on the dead members of their number. Somehow reports filtered back of their predicament, and on 4 October the 77th Division was ordered

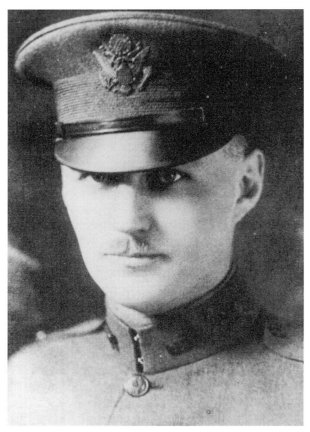

Lt Harold E. Goettler, MoH. 50th Observation Squadron.

Lt Erwin E. Bleckley, MoH. 50th Observation Squadron.

Goettler and Bleckley's de Havilland DH.4.

Ground panel markers used for air-to-ground communications, being laid out. It also helped the airmen to identify friend from foe.

into the area to try and relieve them, but were driven back by the Germans. Aircraft then tried to deliver food and ammunition by air-drop, but this failed miserably, mainly because the exact location of the battalion was not known. Three aircraft from the 50th Observation Squadron searched for the battalion, two of which were shot down. Both crews survived and managed to return to their base. The third crew, Lt Harold Goettler (pilot) and Lt Irwin Bleckley (observer), thought that they had seen the battalion and went back for a second sortie. They did not return. Their crashed aircraft and bodies were found near Binarville by American ground troops. They were later awarded the Medal of Honor posthumously

for their heroic efforts.

On the morning of 7 October 1918, three more aircraft from the 50th Observation Squadron went out on a search pattern to try and locate the 'Lost Battalion'. This time, after repeatedly diving and making low-level runs through heavy archie and small-arms fire in the suspected area, one of the aircraft, flown by Lts Maurice Graham and James McCurdy, saw a marker set out on the ground. The pilots immediately rushed the location back to the Division PC and at 1800 hours the 82nd and 28th Divisions fought their way through the German lines to rescue the 308th. Of the 463 men in the 308th, 69 had been killed and 159 wounded, and all the survivors were complete-

12th Aero Squadron pilots pose in front of a Salmson 2-A2.

ly exhausted after 5 days of being subjected to relentless rifle and mortar fire by the Germans.

With the gradual retreat of the German Army gathering momentum, the opposite was happening in the air. The German Air Service became more concentrated and began to offer greater resistance to the Allied aircraft. The Fokker D.VII was far superior to the SPAD and, together with the hardened veteran pilots from the various *Jastas,* began to take their toll of the Allied aircraft flown by less experienced pilots of the 2nd Pursuit Group. No. 22 Squadron alone lost nine pilots in the following two months, while the 2nd Pursuit Group as a whole lost forty pilots – thirty-one killed and nine taken prisoners-of-war. The only bit of light in this period of darkness was that from the end of September to the middle of October the USAS had shot down over 100 enemy aircraft and more than 20 observation balloons.

As the Americans pushed forward, other problems manifested themselves. The heated battles on the ground were taking their toll on men and supplies; consequently, infantry units within the divisions, because of losses, were being amalgamated with other depleted units. Among these various infantry units had been air liaison officers who had kept in constant touch with their counterparts in the aero squadrons. They also had a good working knowledge of the divisions' strengths, weaknesses and tactics, and also understood the need for communication with each other. When some of these officers were killed or moved to another sector and a new unit formed, there was always the possibility that the new unit would have no one who had had previous contact with an aero squadron.

When the third phase of the Meuse–Argonne offensive got underway, this problem was highlighted when the 50th Observation Squadron was assigned not only to support the 77th Infantry Division, but also the 1st and 12th Observation Squadrons who were flying photographic missions. The 77th had no one who had any knowledge of air liaison and had rapidly to assign one of their officers to the task. This, as one can imagine, caused numerous problems, but fortunately none that was insurmountable. Even the balloon units did

General Mitchell on a visit to the Escadrille Lafayette.

not find themselves immune to this problem. They too found themselves being shifted along the Front as the offensive gathered momentum, only theirs was a slightly different problem. Their trained observers and telephone operators were hard to replace when either killed in action or suffering from influenza (an epidemic that was at the time sweeping across the country) or dysentery, and their services spread increasingly thinly over a larger area. Infantry units could be relieved and given respite, but the balloon units had no such luxury available to them. In fact, when the weather prevented them from launching their balloons, instead of resting they were split into teams of stretcher bearers and sent into the wood and no-man's-land to find wounded soldiers and take them back to clearings where ambulances would be waiting.

Despite the advance by the Allies things did not get any better, and in the middle of

October General Pershing became General of the Armies when the 2nd US Army was formed under the command of General Robert Bullard, while 1st US Army was commanded by General Hunter Liggett. Colonel Milling became Chief of the Air Service for 1st Army, while Colonel Lahm assumed command of 2nd Army's Service, and General Billy Mitchell became Chief of the Air Service for both armies. Now came the problem of dividing the air units between the two armies and General Mitchell issued a directive to all concerned: 'The duties of the Chiefs of the Air Service of the armies are, primarily, to see that the aviation assigned to the armies works in the closest possible liaison with the troops on the ground. Every effort will be made to make this a success, particularly with the staffs, infantry and artillery.'

The 1st Pursuit Group comprised four squadrons – the 27th, 94th, 95th and 147th –

135th Observation Squadron. L-R Rear: Schlesinger, Coleman, Stewart, Bromley, Smart. L-R Front: Fleet, Clarke, Landon, Stoner, Hart.

together with the 91st and 135th Observation Squadrons, and the 2nd Pursuit Group was made up from the inexperienced 13th, 49th, 22nd and 139th Pursuit Squadrons and assigned to the 1st US Army. The 1st and 12th Observation Squadrons were added later, together with the 1st, 2nd and 4th Balloon Companies. The 2nd US Army was assigned the 85th, 168th and 258th Observation Squadrons together with the 8th and 354th Observation Squadrons. After some debate the 135th Pursuit Squadron was reassigned to the 2nd Army and attached to the 4th Corps. To increase the number of squadrons to be assigned to the 2nd Army, the AEF requested that the 17th and 148th Pursuit Squadrons be released from duties with the RFC. The British agreed to the request, but refused to allow the

Sopwith Camels used by the squadrons to return with them. This was not out of a fit of pique, but simply that they themselves had suffered a number of losses of both men and aircraft and could not afford to lose the latter. So both American squadrons arrived at Toul without aircraft and joined up with the 25th Pursuit Squadron, who had recently arrived at the Front – but had no aircraft.

The French were pressurised into providing aircraft for the three squadrons, and agreed to provide SPADs. This of course meant that the pilots had to go through yet more transitional training, which was not completed until the first week in November. Colonel Lahm was angry about the delay, because it meant that the only protection for the 2nd Army's Observation Squadrons lay with the 141st

Lt J.R. Stacey, USAS, getting into a Sopwith Dolphin of No. 85 Squadron. Stacey was a Chief of the Iroquois tribe and five other associated tribes. He was killed in a crash in 1918.

Pilots of No. 85 Squadron, USAS. L-R: Lt Augustus Horn; Lt Lewis F. Turnbull and Lt Lawrence B. Loughran.

Lt J.O. 'Jessie' Creech of the 148th Aero Squadron, USAS, giving the victory sign after returning from a sortie.

Pursuit Squadron, and they could only give limited cover because they were carrying out patrols and strafing missions in addition to their protection flights.

The 3rd Pursuit Group, comprising the 93rd, 213th and 28th Pursuit Squadrons, had been a plan of General Pershing's for some time. While the 93rd and 213th Pursuit Squadrons were already stationed at Vaucouleurs, the 103rd had been prepared to move since 29 July. Major Thaw, who had headed up the 103rd Pursuit Squadron ever since the *Escadrille Lafayette* had been absorbed into the squadron, was relieved of his command and replaced by Captain Robert Rockwell, a former member of the Lafayette

B Flight, 148th Squadron, USAS. L-R: Lt Percy Cunnius; Lt Sidney Noel; Lt Elliot White Springs; Lt Larry Callaghan; Lt Orville Ralston; Lt Harry Jenkinson.

Charles Nungesser (centre) visiting with members of the Escadrille Lafayette. On the left of the picture is Norman Prince and on the right Didier Masson.

Major Huffer's SPAD at the German airfield at Metz.

Flying Corps. The 103rd had fought under four different French Army commands up to this point and was temporarily assigned to the 2nd Pursuit Group, but later assigned to the 3rd Pursuit Group. Major Thaw, in the meantime, had moved to Vaucouleurs to take charge of the 3rd Pursuit Group. With all these moves came a lull in activity which was to last the month of August. The 3rd Pursuit Group was then moved north to Lisle-en-Barrois, and some of the fiercest air activity they had ever encountered. The German backs were now against the wall and they were fighting for every inch of ground and air space.

Among the members of 93rd Pursuit Squadron was Lt Oscar Gude, the squadron's flight commander. He had been the subject of a great deal of scepticism and criticism over the previous months regarding his moral fibre. This arose from an incident on 19 May when, after exhausting his ammunition on long-range passes, his engine allegedly 'ran rough' (this

wasn't the first time he had claimed this problem) causing him to return to base just before his patrol encountered an overwhelming hostile enemy fighter patrol. His aircraft, SPAD No. 15219, always seemed to be out of commission whenever missions were needed, causing a great deal of discontent among the other pilots. On 22 October 1918, Major Huffer, commanding officer of the squadron, ordered Gude on an offensive patrol and when Gude said that his aircraft was again out of commission, Huffer ordered him to take his aircraft, SPAD No. 7662. The following report gave rise to a great deal of speculation:

> On the 22nd a patrol of eight planes, under the command of Lt Wright, set out on a patrol [over] the east bank of the Meuse in the region of Fontains. The leader observed an enemy biplane coming from Germany. With Lts Follmer and Hartman, Lt Wright engaged the

Close-up of the 93rd Pursuit Squadron SPAD after Lt Gude, USAS, had landed it on the German airfield at Metz. Gude claimed he had run out of fuel.

enemy in combat. The fight took place in a teeming rainstorm and they arrived back at the airdrome wet and happy. Lt Gude failed to return from this patrol. When last seen he was flying towards Germany.

A few days after the Armistice, a number of Air Service pilots visited a German fighter unit near Metz. Lt Jeffers was shown a photograph by one of the German pilots of Major Huffer's SPAD with several German flyers around it. They said that an American pilot had landed the aircraft on the field and told his captors that he had run out of fuel. The German pilot told Jeffers that when they checked the aircraft there had been plenty of fuel in the tanks. What happened to Lt Oscar Gude after the war has never been established, but his actions seem to endorse the suspicions long held by many of his fellow American pilots.

In the middle of all this Major Marr was

relieved of command of the 94th Pursuit Squadron and replaced by Captain Eddie Rickenbacker. This was a popular move, as Major Marr was not liked by his fellow pilots, but Rickenbacker was, and he set about raising the morale of the squadron immediately. Within days the whole squadron was moved to Rembercourt, only twenty-one miles from the front line. As the Allied armies pushed forward, so did the lines, and a forward base was set up near Verdun with the 27th Pursuit Squadron under the command of Capt. Jerry Vasconcells. The 94th's role was mainly as protection for the advancing Allied troops, but on days when there was very little aerial activity they were assigned to ground-strafing the retreating German Army.

The 4th Pursuit Group was formed under the command of Major Charles Biddle and comprised the 17th, 25th 141st and 148th Pursuit Squadrons. The 17th and 148th had recently returned from operating with the

RFC, where they had been flying combat missions since August 1918, and were probably the most experienced squadrons in the USAS.

The 1st Day Bombardment Group, now supplemented by the arrival of the 166th Bombardment Squadron, faced its hardest battle on 4 November 1918. On a mission to bomb Cheveney-le-Château, the 96th Bombardment Squadron was intercepted by fifteen Fokker fighters and during the skirmish two of the enemy aircraft were shot down. The same day, thirty aircraft from the 11th, 20th and 166th Bombardment Squadrons joined together in an attack on the same target. They were attacked by eighteen enemy aircraft and lost three bombers. The number of enemy aircraft destroyed has never been recorded, but it is believed that the bombardment squadrons gave a good account of themselves. This was the last time the squadrons had contact with the enemy, as bad weather closed in and kept the aircraft grounded until after the Armistice had been signed.

One of the last two bombing squadrons to come to the Front, the 100th Bombardment Squadron, arrived at Ourches on 1 November. They had extensive training in England at various RFC airfields, and by the time they reached the Front were, in their own words 'ready to the last man to bomb the Boche'. But the Armistice was signed before they could even take off in anger. They had had their share of the war when they and the 155th Bombardment Squadron had embarked aboard the liner SS *Tuscania* in America back in April. Just off the Irish coast, the ship had been torpedoed by a German submarine. Sixteen of the 100th Bombardment Squadron ground crew perished in the icy waters, along with 250 more servicemen. The chance to avenge their comrades had eluded them, but it had not been for the want of trying.

The 163rd Bombardment Squadron was in a totally different position to the 155th and the 100th; they had probably the best equipped squadron and the most experienced pilots and observers of them all. Their commanding

officer, Lt Charles M. Kinsolving, had begun the war as a member of *Escadrille* BR117 as a bomber pilot, carrying out a number of bombing missions. Given command of the 163rd, he and his squadron were sent to Delouze to prepare for the final push. The airfield was nothing but an empty field when they arrived in October 1918, and nothing was spared to make an efficient operational station. The squadron took off on its first patrols on 5 November and scoured the trench areas, but the Germans had retreated, leaving the areas empty. Occasionally enemy aircraft were spotted, but they did not want to engage the American aircraft and usually scuttled out of sight.

By 5 November 1918, the German counter-offensive had fizzled out and their lines were in total disarray as they retreated. The 3rd Pursuit Group had moved up to Faucoucourt, known locally among the pilots as 'Fokker Bend' as the SPAD, although a very good aircraft for the role of bombing and strafing, was no match for the Fokker fighter. On 8 November on one of the bombing runs on a German airfield at Gibeny, four pilots from the 93rd Pursuit Squadron dropped their bombs and were rewarded with one of the most dramatic explosions and pyrotechnic displays of the war as one of the largest of the German ammunition dumps exploded. Also on 8 November orders came to bomb Metz, but as the squadron prepared for their first bombing mission, the weather closed in preventing any flying. Three days later at 1100 hours on 11 November, the Armistice was signed and the war in Europe was effectively over. The aircraft had just been wheeled from their hangars when the news of the Armistice came through. The bomber aircraft were pushed back inside for the last time.

There were other squadrons that arrived too late for the war, such as the 41st, 138th and the 638th Pursuit Squadrons. The 638th became operational at the end of October 1918 and the 41st on 11 November, and neither saw any action. The 138th Pursuit Squadron had embarked for the Front at the end of 1917, but were diverted to Fort Sill, Montrose, Scotland, to take over the work of the RFC's flying maintenance work. As the final push against the Germans in November 1918 increased, the squadron was sent to Lay St Remy to join up with the 41st and 638th Observation Squadrons, but like them they had arrived too late.

At the end of the war, General Mitchell had forty-five combat squadrons under his command, two of which – the 148th Pursuit Squadron and the 17th Pursuit Squadron – had spent most of the war serving with the RFC on the British Front. In just over two years, the United States Air Service had risen from relative obscurity into a powerful force that, even in the short time of its existence, had left an indelible mark on the world of military aviation. It was the forerunner of what was to become one of the most powerful air forces in the world.

Appendix 1:
PoW Escape Reports

The following are escape reports and reports of life as a PoW from American airmen who were either shot down or crash-landed behind enemy lines.

1st Lieutenant George W. Puryear, USAS. 95th Aero Squadron

Lieutenant Puryear, it is believed, was the first American officer to escape from captivity in Germany, and a narrative of his experiences is one of vigour and youthful audacity. From the time of his capture, partly due to his own eagerness in a moment of success, he made it his aim to escape from the clutches of the Hun, and in the face of tremendous obstacles he accomplished his purpose.

On 14 July, having completed his training in the United States, then at Issoudon and Cazeaux, and having served for two months as a ferry pilot, he was ordered to join the 95th Aero Squadron of the 1st Pursuit Group. At that time the 95th was changing over from the Nieuport Type 28 machines to SPADs, and on 18 July from the Saints aerodrome, Lieutenant Puryear made his first flight over the Château-Thierry sector. With a week of patrol experience behind him, he went up with four other SPAD Scouts to patrol the lines from Château-Thierry to Neuf-le-Château. It was a day of mist and rain, so thick that two of the machines turned back. The other three had an engagement with a German biplane machine, but Lieutenant Puryear ventured on alone in spite of the bad weather. The Hun observer was shot and the pilot forced into a landing. Puryear, in the enthusiasm of probable victory, followed the German plane down, shooting continuously, and thinking himself in Allied territory he landed not far from the wrecked Hun.

As he taxied around the field in his plane he suddenly realised that he might be behind German lines, so he headed his machine round to face the long way of the field and prepared to take off. As he was running up into the wind the machine struck a ditch and nosed over. In the distance behind him and around him, machine-guns were snapping; overhead he saw the white puffs from the bursts of other aircraft barrage, but still he was undecided as to his location. He jumped from the cockpit of his own machine and hunted around for the other planes. The German pilot, in the meantime, had pulled his dead observer out of his aircraft and taken him away. By a gradual process of assessment Puryear became convinced that he was behind German lines and somewhere near machine-gun emplacements.

The first man he saw was an unarmed German who accosted him in a friendly manner. As the man spoke French and wore no helmet, Puryear was suddenly taken with the idea that the man was an Italian. The American asked where he was. The Hun told him civilly the thing that he feared, namely that he was within German lines, and asked him if he was an American officer. Puryear replied that he was, whereupon the German saluted him at attention. A crowd of Germans then began to gather about him from various sides (presumably a German observation balloon had telephoned, warning of his descent) and he was taken captive.

He was conducted straight away to a house which was being used as an emergency hospital, where he was relieved of his flying suit, belt, goggles and other leather equipment except for his helmet, which was taken later, and searched for firearms. During the search he chatted in English with the officer in charge. From this point he was put through a series of quizzes by intelligence officers who sought to enhance their knowledge of Allied aviation by every sort of question. Four different times he was quizzed, and on each occasion in a separate office, but of all the questions the only one he considered to have any particular importance was the enquiry as to where his aerodrome was located.

After these inquisitions he was placed with two hundred prisoners (including two French officers) in a temporary concentration camp, where he was given his first German meal. The meal consisted of old German bread, soddy and stiff like a piece of bacon, and so unappetising that he was unable to eat it although it was then about noon and he had had nothing but a cup of coffee since the time when he had tumbled out of bed in the morning and started from his aerodrome at five a.m. Thus he hungered until six o'clock in the evening when a German soldier in the guard house gave him some barley soup and some horse meat, which his fatigue from marching flavoured sufficiently for him to call it good. There was here a private who was a German–American, quite familiar with Broadway and Brooklyn Bridge. The Hun treated him quite well, but food was scarce and unappetising. That night, as he looked outside, he estimated his chances of getting away, and though he did nothing at that

time, he began to make his plans for escape which culminated in the bold venture of 6 October that opened the way to freedom.

The next morning he was taken along for an all-day march on a meal of so-called coffee, made from brown barley, and some unappetising bread. Upon reaching another town he was engaged by a third in the series of German intelligence officers who, after questioning him, told him in English that he would now be conducted to his 'room and bath'. The 'room and bath' were found to be an old barn with an insufficient layer of straw gathered in one corner. Here he seated himself and fed himself jam and bread, a type of potato bread which Puryear characteristically referred to as a 'clod of dirt', and finally went to sleep with a chill creeping up his back.

The following day he joined a large detachment of prisoners which included 400 French and 80 British, mostly Hospital Corps men, and 28 Americans who had been captured from the 26th and 42nd Divisions during the Château-Thierry fight. The march to Laon which followed was one fraught with discomfort and suffering for many of the men. Puryear, although still possessing his officer's suit with insignia, was lightly clad, and during the night of the 28th would have suffered much but for the generosity of a British Hospital Corps soldier who gave him food and a blanket. To add to his difficulties his shoes wore through during the long tramp and his feet became sore. It was during this trip he first made the acquaintance of Adjutant Andre Conneau, a French pilot, with whom he was to make his first attempt to escape.

The treatment of the prisoners on this long trip was one to aggravate them and beat down the morale. On the way Lieutenant Puryear made friends with 1st Lieutenant Zenos Miller, who had been a pilot in the 27th Aero Squadron of his own group, and with the following lieutenants: Willard Bushey, Crawford J. Ferguson, H.W. Shea and Oats. Between them the men continually complained, 'kicked', swore and precipitated arguments with the more conservative members of the group about their philosophy of accepting the hardships of war with equanimity. Around them the men saw German wounded lying without care, as if they were so many dead horses; a country savagely devastated by the wastes of war; British captive soldiers, starved, pale and unshaven, toiling for the Huns behind their lines, brutally discriminated against, and a few solemn-looking French civilians. The atmosphere was anything but encouraging.

The next day, which was the third on starvation rations of soup and bread, they took a train into Germany, starting at five a.m. and arriving next day at eleven p.m. at Rastatt, Baden, where they were quartered in an old fortress overnight, and then inducted into the Friedrichsfeste camp. There they first received passable food, which came via the British Red Cross. This food was distributed, after being inspected and checked by the Germans, by an American prisoner designated to issue it according to his own methods. At this point they discovered that they were only 160 kilometres from the Swiss border; already strongly urged by a desire for freedom, Lieutenant Puryear made a mental calculation of the number of days' travel that would be necessary to carry him to the border in case he should escape. He estimated that he could do it in between seven and thirteen days.

On the following day he discovered an easy way to get out of the camp. The method, so far as the writer knows, still remains a secret in the minds of those who employed it. As Lieutenant Puryear gave this story to the interviewer prior to the Armistice, he desired to keep secret the means of escape in order that he might do nothing that would reveal to the Germans how a number of Americans had found their way out of Rastatt prison. Puryear decided to couple his chances with those of Conneau the Frenchman, who, he said, looked mean, hard and game enough to do anything, and together they planned escape. Puryear depended upon Conneau, who appeared to have considerable knowledge of the country over

which they were about to travel, and the only preparations which he personally made were to borrow a substantial pair of shoes from a British captain to replace his own, which were in a very dilapidated condition.

On 5 August at 11.30 p.m., Lieutenant Puryear succeeded in making his escape unnoticed. He proceeded to a prearranged spot where he waited for an hour and a half, until after the next change of guard, when Conneau appeared. Together they started on their journey. The Frenchman had a map and compass which they used to guide them, and a heavy French leather and fur coat which he loaned to Puryear from time to time to warm him. After a few hours they entered the Black Forest. At about two o'clock it started to rain, and from that moment it seemed that the heavens never ceased to cast a deluge upon the fugitives. During three nights of travel there were about three hours when it was not raining hard. During the daytime they hid in the forest, resting on the Frenchmen's coat, trying to snatch moments of sleep, but no sooner would they fall asleep than it would start to rain, and they would have to take the coat from under them and crouch beneath it, using it as shelter. The Frenchman was a true comrade, and gave Lieutenant Puryear a full share of what he had. They finally invented the method of thatching themselves in for the day with branches leaning against a tree, a method which succeeded in turning away the rain. After resting by day they would start at 10.30 p.m. when darkness had fallen, and travel onwards.

Conneau, however, was mistaken in his direction and bore too much to the west with the result that they found themselves on the second day still at the edge of the forest, with peasants working quite near them in the fields. Again, on the next night they erred, and at three a.m. on 8 August they came out on the banks of the Rhine. Realising that they were off course they took a small road southwards and, just as they were intending to stop for the day at four a.m. walked into a German sentry on duty. They knew the Rhine was well guarded and the troop concentrations thick, and they were so fatigued and discouraged that they made no attempt to run from the guard. The Hun turned them into the guard house, where they were equipped with blankets and passed a good night in rest. They found that they had been captured 50 kilometres from Rastatt and now, after being rudely thrust into cells for a night's rest at Kehl, they were to be sent straight back to Rastatt. Without any quiz or trial they were sent into confinement for five nights before being transferred to Rastatt.

Puryear was searched and relieved of his helmet. This left him without a hat. The commanding officer of the camp questioned him closely as to his escape and Lieutenant Puryear disclosed everything except the means he had used to get out. Within a short time he was sent with fifteen other American officers to Landshut, Bavaria, where he was assigned to the old castle on the hill north-east of the town which had been set aside as a concentration prison for American aviation officers. There were eighteen of them there, ten of whom were Major Harry M. Brown and his pilots and observers of the 96th Aero Squadron, who had been captured on 10 July after an unsuccessful bombing expedition in thick weather. The newly arrived captives were quarantined and inoculated for cholera, typhoid and smallpox.

The food there was good but meagre. They received meat once a day and white flour twice a week, occasionally pancakes, and although the Red Cross food was excellent they found it scarce. There were no special facilities for entertainment and the days dragged. Under such conditions the minds of the officers often turned towards the chance of escape, but it was now 240 kilometres to the Swiss border, and this, combined with the approach of autumn and its cold nights, was strong persuasion against attempts to escape.

It was a congenial group, however. Among the officers who were there were 1st Lieutenant Carlisle 'Dusty' Rhodes, also of the 95th Aero Squadron, who had been reported dead but had come down in a vrille in Germany, unhurt; Lieutenants H.F. Wardle, Herbert Smith, James E. Lewis and George Ratterman, and Captain James Norman Hall, who had previously been reported dead and was the first American officer captured by the Germans. To pass away the time the men played cards, and an occasional package from home received through the Red Cross added to the comfort of all. The commanding officer of the prison camp was reported by Lieutenant Puryear as being one of the worst of the Huns, a man of mean disposition who 'bawled them out' in German every day by the clock, had their shoes taken away every night at eight p.m., and counted them in their beds with the guard. In spite of this some of the officers planned an escape. They succeeded in getting out by cutting through the wooden wall, but they were recaptured.

Puryear's mind was still bent on escape, but he was wiser than to attempt it here. He applied, therefore, for a transfer to the prison at Villengen. There was in the employment of the Germans a civilian by the name of Pasteur, who had been married to an American girl and who owned property in New York. He was apparently the intermediary between the prisoners and the Germans, and carefully reminded them: 'I am a German, be careful what you say.' Through this individual Lieutenant Puryear made his application for transfer early in September. Major Brown was also transferred. Another lieutenant who had a hole cut through his wall preferred to remain and take his chances of escape. 1st Lieutenant Carlisle Rhodes, who was in the group that had left Landshut, pretended that he was sick and escaped from the train; when Lieutenant Puryear actually became ill, he got no sympathy and nothing but 'hell' from the guards. Lieutenant Rhodes was later recaptured.

Lieutenant Puryear and the party, after two days in stuffy cars – during which time the German guards exercised the strictest rules, forcing them to keep their shoes off, giving them no food for one and a half days and allowing them to go to the toilet only once every five hours – arrived at Villengen. This was a new American officers' camp, fair according to the general standard, but better than others as it developed. It was 15 September when they arrived. The food supplied by the Red Cross was good and the clothing sufficient.

After four or five days Puryear was informed by an interpreter that he had some good news for him. The news was that he was entitled to fourteen days' solitary confinement for his previous escape, and since he had served only five of the days he would be given the pleasure of nine more days in jail. Between 20 and 29 September he languished in a six feet by twelve feet cell with nothing but a bed, table and chair, with a small window above him which let in a few rays of the sun.

He was released on the 29th and by 6 October he had escaped from the camp. In the interim he did considerable figuring. It was 36 kilometres in a direct line to the Swiss border, but to the point to which he later tramped and crossed into Switzerland it was 65 kilometres, and he estimated that he must have tramped a hundred kilometres in order to reach it. But to return to the plans for escape. The Americans had determined upon concerted action, and decided that they would select a night and all attempt to escape from the camp at several points at the same time. Two of them were in such a hurry that eleven others altered their plans and agreed to the same night rather than have their own chances spoiled by the special measures of discipline which which would follow any one attempt. They waited for three nights for plans to develop before making the dash for freedom. Puryear had equipped himself with a hand-drawn map, made by a fellow captive, and a small compass purchased from a Russian officer at a price of one sack of coffee, one box of Red Cross meat, one package of hard-tack and an OD army shirt, the total of which looked like a million dollars to the Russian.

The men had carefully studied the defences of the camp. The barracks were located in an enclosure of about 800 by 200 metres, which was surrounded by a high board fence peaked with barbed wire. Outside that was a wire fence, and still further on, a ditch set with barbed-wire entanglements. The main wire fence was about nine feet tall and on the inside iron hooks were fastened, intended to prevent persons from climbing over it. Both inside and outside the camp powerful electric lights and posts of guards of about one hundred German soldiers, men of some age and limited vigour, were set over the 200 Russians and 77 Americans confined there.

On the night of 6 October, thirteen Americans were waiting impatiently, bent on escape. At 11.15 p.m. the lights flickered and went out (they had been short-circuited by an accomplice who had thrown chains across the wires at a prearranged signal). Apparently there had been some suspicion among the Germans, who were prepared for the trouble; nevertheless, the Americans made their rush from four different points of the camp. Three of the men, including Puryear, had posted themselves in a barracks window on the south side. As the lights went out they pulled from the window its iron grating, which in advance had been carefully cut with a file, and Puryear jumped through to the ground. They had already constructed a fourteen-foot ladder from bed slats, the rungs of which had been fastened in place with wire in the absence of screws. Puryear pulled the ladder through the window and placed it against the fence while Lieutenant Ticknor, a fellow captive, braced it at the bottom. By climbing to the top of this ladder it was possible to jump and clear the main fence, the low fence and the barbed-wire ditch in one leap.

It was a starlit night, but dark. As Puryear scrambled up the ladder it squeaked and aroused the suspicion of the guard who was but ten steps away. 'Halt!' the German guard cried. Puryear was at the top of the ladder. 'Halt!' came the warning cry again. The American jumped, got to his feet and dodged behind a tree four paces away, but the guard had seen him. A second guard was approaching about thirty paces away. Puryear figured that he could not keep one tree between himself and two guards for very long, but a desire to play fair and to still leave a chance for his accomplice, who had not yet jumped from the ladder, made him remain a moment in his place of hiding. Suddenly he ran past but eight feet from the guard. The stolid German followed his instructions and challenged him twice before shooting. The first time the fugitive was three steps away; by the time he could shout again Puryear was ten paces beyond and running a zig-zag course. The German fired and missed. Another shot from the other guard. The bullet whizzed by him in the darkness. On he sped until, at length, just as both guns fired again, he stumbled into a ditch which in the excitement he had forgotten about.

'Forgetting about that ditch probably saved my life,' said Lieutenant Puryear later. 'The Hun thought he had winged me and immediately turned towards the others who were breaking out on every side. There was all kinds of excitement; guns were firing and men were shouting. I heard two more shots behind me, and kept on running until my breath gave out about a quarter of a mile away. I went to a pre-arranged spot where we were to meet, and waited for fifteen minutes, during which time there were about fifty shots exchanged, I should judge. No one came, so I got down on my knees, prayed for luck and started off.'

In his travels towards Switzerland Lieutenant Puryear used the tiny compass which he had received from the Russian. Realising that he would be travelling by night and that it would be difficult to get his directions in the dark he had contrived to make the compass points visible by scraping the phosphorescent material from the face of his wrist watch and applying it to the compass needle. By this means he was able to travel in the dark and still keep himself constantly appraised of his direction. Frequently he heard Germans approaching on the road, whereupon he would step off and into the woods to avoid them, as he was travelling in Russian coat and cap which formed a distinctive silhouette against the sky. One man, who caught him unawares, spoke to him in passing, and Puryear replied '*Gute Nacht*' in his best German.

The journey to the border was without unusual incident. On the night of Thursday, 10 October, he came out south of Walshut about eleven p.m. Believing he was near the Swiss border, he climbed the mountain to assure himself, having seen a picture of the town. The only element between him and freedom was the Rhine. It was only 200 metres across but the current was flowing at a speed of several miles an hour and Lieutenant Puryear had not been in water for two years. He selected a point near a bend where the current would assist in carrying him to the other shore. Then he went into the woods, stripped off all garments but his underclothes and breeches, and gradually crept down to the bank, shedding a garment every few feet. At 5.30 in the morning he sprang into the river and swam it. It was about a fifteen-minute job, but the swift current was so great that eddies and whirlpools pushed him about and very nearly exhausted him before he reached the other side. He crept up the bank, stared back into Germany and cursed it. Several peasants approached, took him into their home and gave him food and clothing, and he was later assisted by the American Red Cross.

Lieutenant Puryear was the first American officer to escape from Germany according to available records, but was in fact preceded by three days by an American private. In general he regarded his treatment in Germany as fair. Men were paid sixty marks a month by the German government, but had to spend fifty-two of this for mess, and with the balance they could buy only two mugs of poor German beer. 'It was an experience,' said he, 'which I am glad I had, but would not go through again voluntarily.'

– from notes taken by L. H. Thayer, 2nd Lt AS

1st Lieutenant William W. Chalmers, USAS. 94th Pursuit Squadron

At 8.30 a.m. on 7 July 1918, I left the aerodrome of the 1st Pursuit Group near Rozoy, France, with a flight of 94th Aero Squadron Nieuports (Type 28) to protect a SPAD biplane machine piloted by 1st Lieutenant William Titus of the 1st Aero Squadron, the objective being a point some twelve or fifteen kilometres north-east of Château-Thierry.

On our second trip to the objective, at about 9.30 and about 4,500 metres altitude, four of us (Lts Coolidge, Meissner, Cates and myself) engaged and shot down in flames an enemy biplane machine. I paused to see the enemy aircraft crash, thinking my friends were still near, but before I could rejoin them I was attacked by two German Fokkers; my motor was damaged by the first burst from their guns. I continued to engage them until my motor was hit again and stopped entirely, and I was forced to land near Peuvarde about fifteen kilometres north-east of Château-Thierry.

German soldiers at once took me prisoner and the two aviators landed and conversed with me for some time in English and German. Then an *Oberleutnant* took me back ten kilometres in a car and turned me over to an intelligence officer, who questioned me in English about the US Air Service in general and the 1st Pursuit Group in particular. As I was naturally reticent he answered most of his own questions and showed he knew almost as much as I did about my own group, its officers, machines, individual records etc. This officer also took my coat, gauntlets, helmet, goggles, uniform, insignia, note-book, USAS identification card and boots – giving me in place of the latter a pair of French wooden shoes.

I then spent a day at Loupeigne, a week in a fortress at Laon, another week at Hisson, and arrived at a prison camp at Kestart on 24 July. I escaped from this camp on the night of 27 July with Lieutenant Geoff Crowns of the 10th Field Artillery, and started south through the Black Forest towards Switzerland, walking at night and hiding during the day. We were captured again at about 10.30 p.m. on 5 August when almost to the Rhine, having passed Neustadt the night before. Two armed soldiers and a civilian made the capture and we were too weak to offer much resistance.

As a penalty I was placed in solitary self-confinement from 6 to 27 August at Rastatt, Karlsruhe and Villengen. From 27 August to 26 November I was given the freedom of the prison camp except for three days in October when I was held under a charge of bribery and found not guilty. Thirteen of us attempted an escape in October, but only three reached Switzerland (Lieutenants Willis and Puryear of the Air Service, and Isaacs of the Navy).

I cannot personally complain of brutal or harsh treatment at the hands of the Germans, though I saw many Allied soldiers, especially the British at Laon, who seemed to be overworked and almost starved. The food given us was insufficient in quantity and of poor quality, but from appearances the Germans were living almost as poorly themselves, and after getting in touch with the American Red Cross we fared very well indeed.

1st Lieutenant Charles R. Codman, USAS. 96th Aero Squadron

Second Lieutenant Charles R. Codman, a pilot of the 96th Aero Squadron, was taken prisoner while on a daylight bombing expedition over Conflans on 16 September 1918. A flight of seven machines started on this expedition, but all but four fell out of the formation before crossing the lines. The remaining four aircraft bombed Conflans, but on the return trip were met by a flight of twenty-four German pursuit planes. Three of the aircraft were shot down in flames while Lieutenant Codman and his observer, 2nd Lieutenant Stewart McDowell, were brought down out of control with one aileron, the rudder and half of the elevator shot off. Both officers were wounded, McDowell seriously and Codman slightly. Codman stated that he shot down three of the enemy aircraft before his machine was brought down, and this awaited confirmation from the statements of three French aviators, also prisoners, who witnessed the fight (the pilots were from the French Squadron C-46).

Lieutenant Codman's aircraft came down in a spiral and crashed in a field near Conflans, in which there were many German soldiers. The aircraft was immediately surrounded. There was no opportunity to set it on fire. The Germans gave first aid to Lieutenant McDowell, and he was taken to hospital. Lieutenant Codman was taken to some barracks in a small town near Conflans. From there he was taken by touring car to an intelligence officer in the neighbourhood of Longuyon. There he was questioned for about three hours. Much wine was brought out. No force was used, and the intelligence officer was most polite. Next morning he was taken to Mont Medy, a prisoners' camp, where he was placed in solitary confinement for three days, and from there he was sent to Rastatt near Karlsruhe and after three weeks at Rastatt was sent to Karlsruhe itself.

In the latter town he spent two nights in the famous 'Dictaphone Hotel' where he was kept with thirty or forty other aviation prisoners, about ten of whom were Americans. Later he was removed to the regular prison camp at Karlsruhe, where he received good treatment and where he stayed about a week. He was then taken to the aviation officers' prison at Landshut, Bavaria. He was allowed to send one postal card on the first and tenth of each month, and a letter on the fifteenth and twenty-fifth. In addition he could send all the picture postcards he desired, and many photographic cards were given to him and the other prisoners as a sort of advertisement for the camp – largely pictures of prisoners drinking or playing games. At Landshut he was inoculated against cholera, typhus and smallpox. He depended almost entirely on the Red Cross for food and had plenty of that. Newspapers were at hand every day.

On 7 November, a revolution occurred in Bavaria and most of the guards were taken away. The revolution, however, was a quiet affair, consisting largely of a political change while King Ludwig was imprisoned in his castle. *Herr* Kurt Eisner, a poet and socialist editor in Munich, was made President of the Republic of Bavaria. The revolution lasted only about two hours. Everything had been planned in advance and many of the old regime officials retained their jobs. There was no saluting of officers in the streets.

Relative to other officers in the camp, the Americans were favoured. Lieutenant Codman stated that this was considered by American prisoners as propaganda for American goodwill after the war. Bavarians disliked the Prussians very much. Treatment at the camp was very good and the food was fairly good, the food situation in Bavaria being better than in other parts of Germany. No rubber or leather goods were to be had. Twenty-four American officers (flying) and a few each of the artillery and infantry were housed in Transnitz Castle, where they were well quartered.

The Armistice came as a relief to the German people of the vicinity, but they were bitter regarding the conditions, considering the paragraph regarding railroad carriages especially unjust.

On 16 November, all the prisoners were taken to Villengen except the Red Cross Committee, who stayed to check the Red Cross material. On this committee, in addition to Lieutenant Codman, were Captain James N. Hall, 2nd Lieutenant R.G. Browning and 1st Lieutenant Henry Lewis. The guards disappeared on this date, and in the evening these four officers left the camp with a German corporal. They spent the night in a hotel in Munich where no one paid any attention to them, and the next day they proceeded by rail with the German corporal to a point on Lake Constance from which they proceeded by boat, landing at Roman's Horn on 17 November. From there they proceeded to Berne, where they spent some days with the

American Red Cross, preparing necessary reports on their committee work. Then they proceeded through Geneva to France, arriving in Paris on 21 November.

1st Lieutenant J.D. Fuller Jr (pilot), USAS. 2nd Lieutenant Virgil Brookhart (observer), USAS. 135th Aero Squadron

On the morning of 12 September, which marked the beginning of the St Mihiel drive, Lieutenants Fuller and Brookhart set out from their aerodrome near Toul on a mission for *réglage* of artillery fire in the vicinity of Mont Sec. The weather was quite unfavourable owing to low, hanging fog and the south-west wind. At a height of 1,500 feet they encountered thick clouds, and after five minutes' progress in a west-to-east direction they became temporarily swallowed up in the clouds. By chasing holes in the clouds they managed to catch glimpses of the various towns over which they were passing. Though this presented some difficulties, since it was their first flight together over the lines, they identified Nancy, and then found themselves over Thiaucourt (west).

They were having such difficulties that they decided to abandon their mission and started south-west with the Ourches aerodrome as a goal. Climbing to 10,000 feet, they proceeded for about half an hour in what they believed to be a south-easterly direction. When they came down they found they were over a range of mountains, and later discovered they had been near Mulhausen. They could see trenches as they neared the ground, and therefore ascended again and proceeded for some time toward the south-west, as they believed, and again came down to find themselves over the front-line trenches. It became apparent to them that a fairly strong wind was blowing them off their intended course. The wind at that time was westerly, and since they had been heading south-west, they concluded that the wind had been forcing them in a southerly direction and at the same time sweeping them constantly with an eastward inclination towards the Swiss border.

Finally they flew below the clouds again, and finding that they had left the trenches behind them they landed. Peasants and soldiers appeared from all directions, and as the country looked strange they took off again with the intention of rising, but the motor died and they were forced to stop and land a second time. People crowded about them. They were not sure just what the trouble was with the motor, but as they had started to rise after the first landing, the Swiss soldiers had fired upon them, and they believed that a bullet had torn the jacket of the motor thus rendering it useless.

The inquiry showed that they were only 600 metres from the border in one of the projections of Switzerland into French territory, and they believed that had they been able to proceed for a few moments longer they would have landed in French territory. The Swiss authorities took charge of the two men and sent them to Berne, and thence to Lucerne. There they were informed of their rights: they could either go free on parole or go to prison. It appears from the statements of both men that they were much chagrined over their internment, and realising that they could not escape while on parole owing to the responsibility of the United States government to surrender them if they broke leave of honour, they preferred to take their chances of escape. Lieutenant Fuller, in particular, stated to the writer that he did not fancy the prospect of being interned in Switzerland for the period of the war, and therefore decided to take his chances in prison with the prospect of escape.

It was agreed, therefore, that Lieutenant Brookhart would go to the hotel at Lucerne on parole, while Lieutenant Fuller would enter the military prison at Andermatt near the St Gotthard Tunnel, where he would reconnoitre the prison, study the chances of escape, and communicate his plans by code in letters to his comrade. It was planned that ultimately Brookhart would also come to the prison and they would escape together.

It happened, however, that by the time Lieutenant Fuller was able to make any substantial plans for escape the prospect of the signing of the Armistice was at hand. Having received no word from his comrade, Lieutenant Fuller decided to make his own escape single-handed. He was on the fourth floor of the prison. Near his cell was a toilet, from which opened a window overlooking the ground below. To this toilet he was ordinarily accompanied by a guard. He made it his habit to stay in the toilet room longer and longer each day, so that his delay on the night of the escape would not excite any suspicion.

The night he chose, in early November, was dark and foggy. He cut his bed sheet into seven strips, which he tied together. These he tucked about his waist, beneath his pyjamas. Immediately upon entering the toilet he fastened one end of the bedsheet rope to the window sill and the other end to his waist. Just as he commenced to let himself down the guard knocked on the door. At the third floor the improvised rope broke and he fell a distance of 30 feet, plunging on to his head and arms. He was severely cut about the face and rendered temporarily unconscious. He recovered consciousness, however, before anyone discovered him, and although lame and sore, he attempted to follow the course of escape which he had mapped out in advance. By careful work he managed to evade the two sentries at the mouth of the tunnel, but in making his way along he lost his candle and matches, on which he had depended to guide himself through the thick fog. As he was coming out of the tunnel he was caught between two sentries, who halted him, took charge of him and turned him over to the authorities. For more than a week he was confined to bed, recovering from the injuries he sustained in his fall. Later he was released upon the signing of the Armistice.

2nd Lieutenant Oscar Mandell, USAS. 148th Pursuit Squadron

Lieutenant Mandell, while serving with the 148th Pursuit Squadron on the British Front, was shot down by ground fire and captured by the Germans. On the morning of 2 September, 1918, he started from the aerodrome at Remesnil with four other machines for an offensive patrol over the lines. There was considerable ground haze with clouds at 2,000 feet. After patrolling for half an hour they observed a flight of SE.5 machines ground-strafing further along the lines, and nearby a patrol of Fokkers. Meanwhile, the American formation had split up in the fog, but they hung around waiting to jump the Fokkers in case they should attack the Allied planes. Finally they got into a fight. Lieutenant Mandell shot down one plane, and was immediately attacked by two others from the clouds. They got above and he could not outclimb them into the clouds. He spent fifteen minutes zig-zagging around in a circle until ground fire shot up his machine and stopped his engine. He came down seven kilometres beyond the lines, crashing through some telegraph wires.

Two German infantry officers engaged him in conversation. They finally took him to dinner where they sat him down to good food and a bottle of wine and treated him courteously. He was then taken to the regimental commandant, in whose office he waited three hours until one of the German guards bade him, 'Stand up for an officer!' He looked at him and laughed. He was walked to the rear for six hours, but was stopped for a quiz by intelligence officers at three different places. His fatigue and hunger gave the Huns an advantage over him, which they sought to use as a means of prising from him information about Allied aircraft. They would order a fine meal, place it before him and then try to get him to talk. When he refused to reveal his country's secrets, they would remove the meal.

Altogether, Lieutenant Mandell made five attempts to escape, and although none of them was ultimately successful, his persistence and courage constantly kept the Huns on the jump. After two days at Sewarde, where he received good treatment, he was sent to Conde, which was the scene of his first escape. With a British officer by the name of Donaldson (Donaldson was in fact an American officer attached to a British squadron) he climbed through a window and dropped fifteen feet to the ground. They travelled rapidly and soon made their getaway to the lines. En route, about three a.m. one morning, they came across a Hun aerodrome located at La Sentinel, south of Valenciennes. They were suddenly struck with the notion of trying to take out one of the German machines and flying it back to their own territory. They found an Albatros two-seater in a tent hangar and immediately got to work to get it out. They cut the canvas the full length and stripped it from the machine, but they were confronted by the difficulty of releasing it from a series of cables which held it in place. They worked on the job for nearly an hour, tinkering with the machine, loading and testing the guns and preparing the ship for an immediate flight when they were able to release her.

By this time, however, it was four a.m. and a German mechanic came whistling down the field, ready to start his morning task of preparing the machine for the Hun fliers. The bold captives still had one cable to remove from the wheel of the landing gear. Upon seeing the mechanic, Mandell, who spoke good German, remarked in that tongue, 'Ah, here is someone to help us.' The mechanic, however, was not to be disarmed by the remark and immediately became suspicious. The two officers approached him and Donaldson seized him by the arms. The Hun struggled in the grasp of his enemy and pulled a small dagger from its scabbard. Lieutenant Mandell now jumped into the conflict and tripped the Hun, but could not prevent him from jabbing Donaldson in the back with the dagger. The German jumped up with an agile movement, and started down the field for help. The officers knew better than to

pursue him after the first five steps, and made their getaway.

'It was a damn shame,' said Lieutenant Mandell in an interview with the writer, 'for we had the machine all trimmed up and the guns all set, and we were going to run the ship up and down that aerodrome and clean out the whole bunch. As it was, we made a getaway.'

The officers hurried along and got through the German lines to the edge of the water where the Germans had inundated the land in the Douai salient. They were about to swim the overflown river, after six days in an energetic pursuit of safety, when a German patrol came along. They laid down in the dark and prayed for luck. Luck was in the air, but it went to the Germans, who nearly stumbled over them. They were recaptured, sent back to Fresnes, court-martialled and given fourteen days' solitary confinement. They were now attacked by another intelligence officer, who discussed the war in its larger aspects and informed Mandell that Germany was preparing to send a delegation to Japan to procure her assistance in case the United States became troublesome.

On 26 September Lieutenant Mandell escaped again with four others. Three of them started towards the Belgian border, but Mandell, in company with a British corporal, made for Holland. They swapped their flying clothes with the French and Belgians, who entertained them royally and secreted them by night. But again luck was on the other side, and as they were passing over the Dutch border they were intercepted.

Then Mandell was sent to Aachem, where he spent four days, then to Karlsruhe for three weeks, then to Landshut, where he left on 15 November for the officers' camp at Villengen. After three days there he was released and came back through Switzerland, where the trainload of American prisoners received a wonderful reception.

The three other attempts at escape were very unsuccessful compared to the first two. In the interim he used to keep a little compass in preparation for future attempts, and when searched would carry it in his mouth. Regarding treatment, he stated that although he was occasionally subjected to insults, it was on the whole pretty good. Red Cross food and packages of Red Cross gifts were received frequently.

2nd Lieutenant J.O. Donaldson, RAF. Att. 32nd Squadron

I was taken as prisoner to Douai, and kept one night, but due to the heavy shelling by the English I was transferred the next day to a temporary prison at Conde. During the evening another American pilot was brought to the prison camp. This American, Lieutenant Mandell, and I escaped that night by jumping out of the second-storey window of the prison and walking through the town. After walking all night, and about two hours before daybreak, we came to a new German airdrome. After making sure that there were no guards guarding this airdrome, Lieutenant Mandell and I attempted to steal a machine. After about two hours' work we managed to get a machine almost entirely out of its hangar, but finally had to take the whole hangar down to get the machine clear. Just as we were about to start the machine, a German came out for early-morning flying. We immediately got into a tussle with him, and during the tussle he stabbed me in the back and slashed up Lieutenant Mandell's clothing quite a good deal, but did not touch him, and we finally hit him on the head with a big electric lamp and ran across the airdrome.

We were not followed, and at the first French house we asked them to take us in. They dressed my wounds for me and gave us food for two days. At the end of the second day, German soldiers were to be billeted in this house, so we had to move on, and although my wound was quite stiff, after once getting on my feet I could walk all right. After a number of adventures and being halted by sentries about eight or nine times (but due to Lieutenant Mandell's being able to speak German, he answered the sentinels as if he were a German officer passing, and we passed safely), on 9 September we passed through all the German front-line trenches and stayed in a shell hole in front of their front lines all day. We could see the English guns firing from where we were.

Between us and the English lines there was a small stream dammed up at one end by the Germans. That night, on trying to wade across the stream, we found it too deep and came back, and we were taking off our clothes to swim the stream when we were caught by a German wiring party on the front of their front line. They carried us back to Battalion Headquarters. The German NCO who captured us was recommended by the battalion commander for an Iron Cross for catching us. After going through Division Headquarters, Corps Headquarters and Army Headquarters we were finally taken to Valenciennes. We were turned over to our old prison, but the guard refused to take us. Apparently they were afraid we would try and escape again, so they sent us to another prison across the street, where we were placed on bread and water for fourteen days.

On the eleventh day, Lieutenant Mandell and I started to think of a means of escape. The only way we could get out of the building below was by passing through the roof. At the end of three days we had a hole sufficiently large for a man to pass through, and on the same day two other Americans came into the camp, Lieutenants T.E. Tillingham and R.A. Anderson. That night all four American officers and one British NCO, Corporal George Rodgers, crawled through the hole in the roof, down into the courtyard, over a wall on the other side, swam the canal and set out across country for the Holland border. We travelled for eight days, travelling in the night and sleeping in the daytime, getting food from friendly Belgians.

On the eighth day we struck Brussels and met some rich Belgians who could speak English. Here we were supplied with civilian clothes, maps and other little details that helped us on our journey. After staying two days in Brussels and looking over the air-dromes, but finding them too closely guarded to take a machine, we went out across country again to the Holland border. About twenty days from the time we left the prison we struck the Holland border. After reaching the border we were unable to cross for nine days. A friendly Belgian supplied us with insulated wire cutters and also told us the exact location of the electric wire. Two days later we crawled up within 10 yards of the wire, but due to the bright sunlight we had to be very slow. It took us three hours to crawl to the edge of the wire, and as soon as the sentinel had come to the edge of his beat and went down the other end, we went up and cut the three lower strands of the electric wire. As soon the sparks had ceased to come out of the wire, we ran across the wire and at the same time the German sentinel yelled and Lieutenant Tillingham claims he fired a shot.

In Holland we proceeded to Rotterdam, and from Rotterdam to Le Havre, and from Le Havre back to England again. The total time we were in Belgium was about twenty-eight days. Two of the others, Corporal Rodgers and Lieutenant Mandell, departed from us at Brussels so only three of us escaped into Holland. The other two, we believe, are still somewhere in Belgium (dated 11 November 1918).

2nd Lieutenant Howard C. Knotts, USAS. 17th Aero Squadron

The following narrative, while only partly in the language of Lieutenant Knotts, has been certified to be authentic in its essential respects, and it is believed it will be found to be of considerable interest and value to the Air Service, both with reference to the completion of data concerning the treatment of our officers while prisoners in the hands of the enemy, and also concerning the abominations committed by the enemy which may be considered important for presentation to the present Peace Conference.

Lieutenant Knotts was a pilot in the 17th Aero Squadron, attached to the 15th Wing, Royal Air Force, British Expeditionary Forces, and was stationed at the time he was captured near the town of Sombrin, France (Pas de Calais). He was detailed for a ground-strafing expedition and left the airdrome at about one o'clock in the afternoon of 14 October 1918, in a Sopwith Camel Scout plane. The engine of his machine was damaged by machine-gun fire and he was obliged to descend near Colombes. He purposely descended at the point which he selected for the reason that it was within the zone of concentrated artillery fire, which he knew would soon damage his machine, making it unfit for further use. At that time he had nothing at his disposal to destroy it; therefore, he did not descend into the zone of safety, which he could otherwise have reached with ease. This point was three or four kilometres beyond the enemy lines in their territory.

He then planned the best manner in which to reach the British lines, and attempted the practically impossible feat of negotiating the Allied shell-fire. He waited for available opportunities between shell bursts and walked and ran from point to point towards the Allied lines, even crossing the enemy lines into no-man's land where he discovered a sunken road, eight or ten feet deep, running first east and west and then turning parallel to the lines north and south. In accomplishing this portion of the flight he was continually sniped at, and two bullets penetrated his flying boots. he then carefully reconnoitred and attempted to find a place of safety where he could await nightfall. He discovered a shallow parallel dugout in the side of the sunken road whose partition had partly fallen in, making it possible to creep from one to the other, as will appear.

Lt Knotts entered the first of these parallel dugouts, hoping to hide there until nightfall and then cross over to the British lines. He had, however, been discovered in his flight, and noticed soon after he entered the first one a German non-commissioned officer approaching to take him. This German soldier had apparently noticed him enter the first dugout, and he looked cautiously into that one, but in the meantime Lt Knotts had succeeded in creeping over into the other one. He immediately jumped upon the German soldier, who had pulled his pistol, and in the succeeding encounter which developed for the possession of the automatic, the German soldier accidentally killed himself with his own pistol. Other Germans, however, had witnessed the struggle and there ensued a pistol duel between Lt Knotts, armed with the dead German's automatic which still held eight or nine bullets, and four or five Germans similarly armed.

In this encounter Lt Knotts was overpowered by five Germans dropping down from the elevated side of the sunken road upon him in his awkward position. These soldiers stripped him immediately of his flying boots, flying insignia, watch, Sam Browne belt and ring, and a guard of two of them marched him at pistol point to a lieutenant assembling a company in the line. This march was made over shell-shot country strewn with fragments of barbed wire, sharp stones and the usual severe and devastated conditions of a shell-shot country, without shoes, from 3.30 in the afternoon until approximately six in the evening. His feet became torn and swollen on the march so that later he was severely blood-poisoned in one foot and the calf of the leg, the ankle having been slightly wounded by a machine-gun bullet when he was shot down.

He was immediately marched in charge of a guard of soldiers to Divisional Headquarters, seven kilometres away. There were signs and other evidence that indicated that this was possibly the 33rd German Division. Here a German captain, who could not talk English, attempted to interview him, an attempt which failed. Then he was interviewed by a poor interpreter, but Lt Knotts refused to talk. It should be stated here that he had in his possession a flat purse with his identity card and

about one hundred and forty francs in notes, and a deposit slip from a British bank, which the Germans had overlooked in the examination of his clothes. He carried nothing else. With the money which he retained in his possession he managed to bribe his German guard to purchase a pair of well-worn shoes for him. During this interview he was threatened and browbeaten by his interviewer who insisted that he must have carried secret papers and a British flying map, which they particularly wanted to find.

At approximately 6.30 p.m. he was marched by one mounted uhlan, sometimes at the point of a revolver and at other times when the guard was changed at the point of a set lance, until approximately three o'clock in the morning without any food from the time of his capture. At this time he reached Maresches, France. His march was accomplished by four reliefs of guard and was made unnecessarily long because of its circuitousness. Lieutenant Knotts was particularly familiar with this country, and is able to state precisely his eastern route which led to the outskirts of Valenciennes and thence south-east to the town of Maresches, where Corps Headquarters for that Front was located. He is unable to state which corps this was. Here he was taken to the Hotel de Ville and ushered into the presence of a brigadier-general who was in bed. This officer could speak a little English and insisted on Lt Knotts answering certain questions which would identify his unit. He also insisted that he must have secret documents and a map. Lt Knotts replied to this general but gave him no information whatever. This so incensed him that he peremptorily ended the interview and ordered Lt Knotts to be taken to an intelligence officer. This was promptly done. The corps intelligence officer was in the same building. He spoke English fluently. Lt Knotts was here searched again and his pocket book, which was the only thing he carried in his clothing, was discovered. This interview was as futile as the other.

During the interview Lt Knotts had noticed

plenty of food and hot tea at hand, and although he was asked if he had eaten, he was denied any of it. From here he was taken to the quarters of non-commissioned officers. They were in a state of carousal and desired to prove to him that they had plenty of food, with the result that he had an excellent meal contributed to by many of the soldiers from their own rations. Here he got good treatment for the rest of the night, a comfortable bunk being improvised. Lt Knotts discovered that this guard comprised Prussian Guard troops (this fact might serve to identify the corps). He slept until eight o'clock in the morning.

At that time he was roused and began a march which lasted until three o'clock in the afternoon with an uhlan guard, in a circuitous route which he can identify. He reached St Cast in the vicinity of Bavai at the end of the march. During this march the Germans gave him no food whatever, but a beggar at the roadside gave him a hot baked potato and an apple. At the end of the march he was placed in a typical loft on the second floor of a building filled with German soldier prisoners confined there for mutiny. Lt Knotts is able to state here as a matter of interest that there were approximately one hundred of these soldier prisoners in his building and that practically every available building in the town had large numbers of such mutinous soldiers. It appears that there were so many of these soldiers mutinying daily that it would have been futile to shoot them as fast as they came in.

By this time Lt Knotts' feet were in a frightful condition; moreover, he was hungry. The Germans gave him no rations or medical attention, but one of the prisoners who proved to be sympathetic shared his rations and gave him some salve or grease and bandages which he applied to his feet with considerable benefit. He was imprisoned in that loft for the rest of that day, all that night, and the whole of the next day and night. There were no sanitary conveniences. The place appeared to be free from vermin, however. No attention was paid to him during this time.

In the meantime, five former Australian prisoners who had attempted escape were recaptured and brought to this same loft, from which they, in company with Lt Knotts, were escorted by an uhlan guard to the town of Bavai the next day, approximately five kilometres away. That afternoon they entrained aboard flat cars loaded with airplanes. The flat car that Lt Knotts was on was loaded with new Fokker monoplane fuselages. None of the other prisoners was on this car, but there was a German sentry aboard. The wings of these planes were in the car behind with the five Australian prisoners. As the ride lasted until after midnight, it became pitch dark. The guard had been informed of Lt Knotts' condition and paid very little attention to him, permitting him to move freely about the flat car. During his journey he watched for an opportunity and climbed successively into the cockpits of each of the three Fokkers and succeeded in breaking one of the main cross-bracing struts in each of the fuselages, thus completely crippling the three machines under the very nose of the German guard. Food had been given to the six prisoners, consisting of a can of bully beef and a loaf of bread, but Lt Knotts was not permitted to mingle with the other prisoners on the car behind, and as they carried the bully beef he was unable to obtain any of it. He ate the loaf of bread, which was all the food he had until the end of his journey.

At Peruwelz, Belgium, they detrained and were marched to a supposed main collecting station (*Stallelager*), but this camp had been moved further back due to the rapid advance of the British, and Lt Knotts and the five other prisoners were taken to the railroad station where they spent the night. They proceeded to Mons, Belgium, the next day. No food was provided for this journey. This portion of the trip was made on regular passenger train. Mons was reached that afternoon. From there the six prisoners were marched into the town to an ancient nunnery which had been converted into a collecting station at which there were approximately 200 British enlisted men,

6 British officers and 1 American officer. (This American officer was Lieutenant Walter Avery of the 148th Aero Squadron, attached to the same British wing and operating on the same front as the 17th, Lt Knotts' squadron.)

Here Lt Knotts was separated in a small room with the other officers, the living conditions being fairly good. No bunks or blankets were provided, but the room was comfortably heated by a coal stove with fuel enough provided for a continuous fire. Here the meals were three in number each day. The morning and night meals comprised plenty of German coffee and black bread, and the noon meal was served by Belgian Red Cross workers provided with food by the American Food Commission. This was the fifth day of Lt Knotts' imprisonment, and the first day he was permitted to wash. The Belgian Red Cross were permitted to provide the prisoners with a towel, soap, toothbrush and a package of dentifrice. The sanitary conditions were good.

During this four-day stay, Lt Knotts was taken each day to the quarters of a German Air Service officer who was a flight commander. He had breakfast with him each morning. He told him that his name was Shroeder and there were evidences that led Lt Knotts to believe that this was his real name. This man later proved to be extremely familiar with the personnel, operating conditions and losses particularly of two American squadrons on the British Front and of American officers with British squadrons on the Front – hence Lt Knotts' information concerning officers reported missing or dead which might otherwise be impossible to obtain. He describes this man as about 5ft 7in in height, weighing about 145 lb, with dark brown hair appearing black in the dim light. He was in the habit of wearing his hair as we associate generally with Germans, that is, unparted and close-cropped both sides with the top brushed straight up and the crown graduated to an inch in length, but it is possible that in civilian life or at present he wears his hair differently, as it appeared from a picture he showed to Lt Knotts, taken before

the war, which showed his hair long and brushed back from the forehead. It was a side-view portrait and did not show whether the hair was parted.

This man could not have been over thirty years of age. His eyes were dark and flashing. His complexion was sallow. His nose was aquiline. He was always smooth-shaven in the presence of Lt Knotts. His teeth were white and apparently sound. He could speak perfect English. Whether or not he had lived in the United States is not known to Lt Knotts. He habitually wore a German second lieutenant's uniform with the brevet of an observer and eventually a pilot, but, as is customary in the German Air Service, he still wore the observer's brevet. He wore the ribbon of the 2nd Class Iron Cross and the ribbon of either the State of Bavaria or the State of Hanover on the left breast, and he wore the 1st Class Iron Cross in the usual position, left-hand side below the belt. The state ribbon was yellow and black mounted with gilded-metal crossed sabres. Lt Knotts believes that he must have been a second lieutenant as he stated and appeared to be, for the reason that in many conversations he exhibited chagrin at never having been promoted, notwithstanding meritorious service, as was evidenced by his decorations and many conclusive remarks.

Lt Schroeder's flight was stationed in the vicinity of Mons at this time. He told Lt Knotts that he had served in the German Air Service in Russia during this war. He also asked Lt Knotts whether he had heard of a German flying officer who had flown over the lines in a French machine, disguised as a Frenchman, landing upon a British airdrome, and had taken luncheon with the officers from a British aero squadron. Lt Knotts believed he mentioned the number of the squadron, but inasmuch as he had never heard the story before and considered it fantastic he has forgotten the number, if it was mentioned. This is of note, however, because it corresponds with the facts known to you and others.

This officer also gave Lt Knotts valuable

information concerning the graves of two American flying officers, 1st Lieutenant Lloyd Hamilton and Lieutenant Gerald Thomas, who are buried in the following British Artillery co-ordinates. Upon the map known as France, Sheet 57.C, Edition 2, Scale 1/40,000, Lieutenant Hamilton's grave is north of Lagicourt which is NE of Bapaume, northern France, within the artillery co-ordinates 57.C, 18c; Lieutenant Thomas's grave is located upon Sheet 51.A, Edition 1, co-ordinates 51.A, 28a. This officer fell from a height of 6,000 feet in flames and was completely burned before reaching the ground. Lt Knotts saw this personally on 22 September, so there will be burnt remnants of the machine still there.

Lt Knotts was never able to visit these graves, but feels sure that the information given him is correct because it corresponds with known information. It will be found upon visiting these graves that Lieutenant Hamilton's machine was burnt up. Portions of the machine will undoubtedly be found nearby, according to Lieutenant Shroeder. He had complete information concerning all American flying officers with the British who had been taken prisoner, and also those who had been killed. This is proven because many facts that were related to him by Lt Schroeder at this time previously unknown to Lt Knotts have been verified by Lt Knotts since his return to the American forces. He had a portfolio with him containing the names and full particulars concerning the status of all American fliers then with the British, or who had been taken prisoner, killed or wounded by the Germans, and many others not with the British.

Lieutenant Knotts was not taken to this officer in any sense to be interviewed, but merely through his courtesy. He told Lt Knotts that it was a hobby of his to know everything possible concerning American flying officers and that he was not an intelligence officer; but this assertion would of course be proved untrue if his own statement that he was the German flying officer who had flown in a French officer's uniform to a British airdrome for the sole purpose of obtaining information was correct. Lt Knotts knew nothing else concerning this officer which would be of value to identify him, except that his flight was a two-seater flight comprising various types of machines. He told Lt Knotts that he had one Hannover, two LVGs, two Albatros two-seaters and one Halberstadt. This officer, being a flight commander, was given considerable licence off-duty and lived comfortably in a small, well-furnished house on the edge of the town of Mons, approximately two miles away from the collecting station. Lt Knotts was conducted to this house and returned by a guard for breakfasts during his stay there. He believes that if this officer could be identified and interviewed it would be of the greatest service to complete the investigation of data not now known concerning many of our officers reported missing or killed within the German lines whose graves are known only to him, so far as Lt Knotts knows, unless it be shown that he was really an intelligence officer, in which case it is probable that this data was also forwarded to the German Intelligence Bureau Archives.

At the end of four days' stay here, all the prisoners were moved with the exception of Lt Knotts and the two British boys permanently retained there as cooks since March. Lt Knotts was then transferred to a different room upstairs. Learning from the cook boys that the place was now guarded by a single sentry, and as his room was clumsily locked, he watched for a favourable opportunity that evening and escaped. Having become fairly well acquainted with the general directions during his visits to the house of Lt Schroeder, and having learned of the advance of the Allied lines to a point he thought he could reach by night marches, he struck out in that direction. He was favoured by rain and fog and walked fully fifteen kilometres before dawn, hiding himself in a clump of bushes. Soon after daylight he shifted his position to a better point of vantage, commanding a view of the main road which he had been following that night, and was soon taken prisoner by a German non-commissioned officer into whose arms he almost stepped.

He was promptly returned to the collecting station and interrogated again in the same room from which he had escaped, this time better guarded. He remained here two days longer, during which time several prisoners came in, and then was taken to Soignies where he joined the original group of prisoners from the collecting station at Mons, then in a permanent prison camp known as 'English Prison Camp #19' (*Englander Geflagen Lager #19*). This was a reprisal camp and never a permanent station for very long, and was kept just behind the lines at all times, moving back as the lines moved back, locating in factory towns where buildings that were big enough to accommodate 1,500 prisoners could be found. The one selected here was formerly a tannery. Lt Knotts learned that this was a reprisal camp from the many statements of prisoners who were so informed by the German guard. These prisoners were principally Australians and Canadians who were reputed by the Germans to habitually take no prisoners.

There were 1,500 men at this reprisal camp at Soignies, 800 of whom were housed in a building where the officers were also kept. The sanitary conditions were indescribably vile and in fact continued so from that time on. The food conditions were also intolerable. The meagre rations were weakening and there was no medical attendance. There was but one so-called doctor there for these 800 men, who was actually one of the prisoners, a British stretcher-bearer who knew only the rudiments of first aid and nothing about medicine and surgery. Sicknesses of many different kinds developed. The great majority of the prisoners had dysentery. At night the men were obliged to relieve themselves in the yard or court for exercise, an enclosed space approximately ninety feet square. They begged for permission to dig their own latrines, a request which was denied them. The stench was nauseating and permeated through the tannery. Many of the prisoners

died. No bunks were provided so prisoners slept on the floor packed in like sardines, bodies touching. All the prisoners had body lice. Lt Knotts killed 167 of them from his own undershirt one morning, and about the same number that same afternoon. He states that it was impossible to kill them as fast as they propagated. No means whatsoever for cleaning the clothes were provided.

All this lack of sanitation was unnecessary, for in the town where the camp was progressively located there was always plenty of available German medical skill. At one place the Germans were even preparing to take over the building in which the prisoners were located for a local German military hospital, but no medical assistance was given to the prisoners, even here. At one time Lt Knotts, together with Lt Avery (the other American officer) and the British officers were placed in the meanest, darkest, most unsanitary, damp, cold, unventilated room available in the prison building, for the reason that they refused to sign paroles, the sole advantage of which appeared to have been the promise of a bath. This illustrates well and typically the habitual and inhuman denial of common, civilised, sanitary amenities which were always available to alleviate in some slight manner the miseries of the prisoners.

As a result of this intolerable and weakening treatment which he received in prison from the day of his capture until the early part of November, Lt Knotts' wound became gangrenous and worse until his release on 15 November, at which time he was wholly unable to walk. This state of affairs was preposterous because it could have been avoided from merely elementary assistance and sanitary attention on the part of a doctor whose services could easily have been obtained.

From the time of his incarceration in Soignies until 15 November, Lt Knotts and the other prisoners were frequently marched, as has been stated above, always retreating further and further from the original frontier as it moved back. During these progressive marches the prisoners became weaker and weaker, some of them daily being unable to walk. They had to drag heavy wagons containing the plunder and equipment of a great variety of kinds, and one light military wagon containing food. Twenty-five men were detailed to drag one of these wagons. Sometimes some of the prisoners collapsed and were placed aboard the very carts they were assigned to drag. Their fellows gladly undertook the burden of this additional load. At one place the prisoners managed to obtain a carriage in some unknown manner and dragged these prostrate prisoners into it. The guard was often very brutal. The food wagon contained rations sufficient for every one of the prisoners, but the full ration was never issued, as was later proved. An inspection of the large remaining food stock upon the fourth day of the march, for which five days' rations were loaded into the food wagon, showed nearly half of the issued food remaining. This inspection was personally made by Lt Knotts. On 15 November, the day of his release, none of the remaining food was given to the prisoners, their inhuman guards claiming that they needed it for their journey back to Germany.

From 11 November on there were many evidences of laxity in the German guard towards the prisoners and mutiny towards their own officers. As they proceeded along the road the prisoners passed many German troops, abandoned by their higher officers. They encountered no higher-ranking officer than an *Oberleutnant*. These troops were flying the red flag.

On the last day of imprisonment the group of prisoners with Lt Knotts numbered only 150 to 200. The last day's march was from Maransart, Belgium, to Boucet. The place of their intended release was Holland. They intended to entrain at Liège, five days' march from Maransart. The prisoners were kept off the main roads to avoid encountering the many passing detachments of troops. On the fourth day's march only a half day's rations were issued in the morning, comprising one loaf of bread for seven men – nothing else. At

Boucet the prisoners were released without food or guidance. They were in a country plundered, ruined and terrorised, without resources, were too weak to march further and were left in a local hospital. Five are known to have died owing to their frightful condition. This place was 30 kilometres from Liège, 70 kilometres from the nearest town of Holland (Maasterlink). Brussels was 10 kilometres away. The advancing Allied army was 120 kilometres away (8 or 10 days' march). An English captain took back 150 enlisted men and some British officers to the town of Hurmat, 2 kilometres away. Others left for an unknown route.

Lt Knotts and eight British officers, pitifully weak from their inhuman treatment at the hands of their captors, begged to remain in the barn of the chateau. The owner of the chateau was a Belgian, the *burgomeister* of the town of Boucet, and his wife proved to be of the noblest type of womanhood: sympathetic, humane, generous and courteous. It is believed only just that her gracious assistance to an American officer in distress be recognised officially by a letter of appreciation from the military authorities. It is believed by Lt Knotts that a similar appreciation has already been sent by the British military authorities in acknowledgement of her generosity and ministrations to the five British officers housed at her home with him. The name of this woman is Madame Stanislas Seny Oury.

Here Lt Knotts and the five British officers with him were cared for, nursed and fed just as if they were in their own homes. All the available local medical treatment was provided. Madame Seny herself nursed Lt Knotts, and it must be understood that for three or four days after these officers were taken into her home the Germans were going by there and some ten German officers and 900 enlisted men were being quartered each night in her chateau and barns, so this care was given to the officers at the expense of having the livestock and the provisions of the farm plundered and stolen by the Germans.

During this time, Lt Knotts and the five

British officers had been quartered in the service portion of the barn where heating, bathing and delousing facilities were provided, and also a clean change of under and outer clothing. The only reason these officers were not taken into the chateau proper, as was done afterwards, was because each night of the German evacuation so many German officers were quartered in the house that hardly adequate sleeping accommodations were left for the Seny family itself. After the last of the Germans had gone these officers were taken into the house and were treated as esteemed guests.

No Allied troops came through this vicinity except one French division, and that offered practically no transportation facilities to the prisoners. It did offer them, however, the advantages of the French military post, which was so slow that it brought no immediate results. After a period of three weeks all the British officers had recovered and started back to their army, which was then only 30 kilometres away, but Lt Knotts was still unable to walk any great distance and was obliged to stay on until word was conveyed by letter carried by the gardener of Madame Seny to the American section of the Permanent Allied Armistice Commission. The commanding officer was Major-General Charles Rhodes, American Expeditionary Forces. The day after the letter reached Major-General Rhodes, he sent a car with Captain White of the US Medical Services to Boucet so that Lt Knotts was able to report for duty to the American Section of the Armistice Commission on 9 December 1918.

During his sojourn here he was given skilful medical attention. On 14 December, Lt Knotts was ordered to report back to the 16th American Aero Squadron through the commanding general of the Third Army Wing Headquarters, which were believed to be then at Coblenz. It was known that Lt Knotts would be obliged to collect his personal belongings left at the squadron and probably be obliged to go immediately after that to a hospital before

he was completely restored to health. He proceeded in compliance with his orders to Coblenz, but found that the army commander, Third Army, was at Hayson. Here he received verbal orders which sent him to report to the Army Air Service commander stationed at that time at Trèves (Trier), with which order he complied, reaching General Mitchell's office on 15 December 1918. From here he was ordered to proceed to Toul where he reported to his squadron, which moved the next day from Toul to Colombey-les-Belles. Lt Knotts was immediately sent to Camp Hospital #5 at Bariesy-la-Sete. Here he was obliged to remain for six weeks, and on 26 January 1919 he left the hospital to receive orders for transportation to the United States, which will be issued as soon as he has completed the special duty for which he was ordered to these headquarters.

2nd Lieutenant R.A. Floyd, USAS. Ferry pilot

Lieutenant Floyd, on his first ferry trip from Orly to Colombey-les-Belles, had the extraordinary experience of being lost en route and flying a brand-new Salmson plane into German territory. It was his first flight in a Salmson plane and his first voyage into the Colombey-les-Belles region, with the result that he knew neither his motor nor his maps. He represented that when he reported at Orly, he was formally introduced to the Salmson plane, informed there were some maps in the back seat of the machine and casually told that he should fly it to the First Air Depot. He declared he was unable to obtain from those on duty any special information of the plane or territory he was to fly over, and that he was thus thrown on his own resources.

Under these circumstances he decided to follow another pilot. After some trouble starting the motor he mounted into the air and flew for about an hour in a general easterly direction, but was unable to find the other machine, which had started in advance of him. He returned, therefore, to Orly, for which, he declared, he was severely reprimanded. He set out next day, 23 July 1918, and had considerable trouble in getting to Vinets, which was ordinarily a stopping place for such trips. From Vinets there are two routes to Colombey-les-Belles; of these Lieutenant Floyd took the northern one which ran fifteen to twenty-five kilometres behind the lines, as they existed. Unfamiliarity with the country caused repeated difficulty in finding his way, he said. Being in doubt as to what locality he was over he searched about for the large-scale maps which would show the lines better, but was unable to find them. He kept on north and east, following his maps, for about an hour. It became very cloudy and the mist hung low. He was lost. He decided that he would fly for ten minutes and if he could not then orient himself he would land. He picked out a good field near Worchingenn, Germany, spiralling down to it, and in landing shot over the field. It proved to be a dummy Hun aerodrome. A German soldier, having spied him in the air, had hidden himself in an adjacent wheat field, and when the machine stopped he jumped up thirty feet away and captured him. The landing gear of the machine was smashed, but otherwise the machine was in such condition as it would have been on delivery, with specifications in the rear seat.

Lieutenant Floyd was taken to the aerodrome of a new Fokker squadron where he dined with Germans who sought to discuss with him America's part in the war and showed him considerable knowledge about the American Air Service. He was kidded about Major Brown, who landed the six Breguets in Germany, said Lieutenant Floyd, and was asked 'if our Liberty machines were going to act the same way'.★ Persistent efforts were made by the Germans to get information from the captive. When, on 26 July, no information was forthcoming, they made him take off his Sam Browne belt and confined him for seven days in a cell on German food of execrable variety. His orderly was a New Yorker, fortunately, and occasionally gave him French biscuits which were a small source of nourishment.

He was taken next to an underground fortress at Strasbourg where he met American enlisted men. The enlisted men's food was very poor, and his was hardly better. He received two meals a day from a restaurant nearby and described the food as 'filthy', consisting of barley soup and blood sausages which turned his stomach. At Karlsruhe he was interrogated again, and he lived for some time in the hotel there which was in a filthy condition and plentifully equipped with dictaphones through which the Germans sought information of value.

He finally got to the camp at Landshut. From this camp he made his escape with three others: Lieutenants Doehler, Battey and C.W. Peckham of the RAF. It was a 'ragtime getaway'. For eight days they had worked to cut their way through the barracks door by the removal of certain screws from the panel, and when, at length, they set to make their escape and were lined up on the cornice ready to leap over the adjacent wall, they were discovered. They all jumped together, and amid the ringing of bells, blowing of whistles and shooting of guns they cleared the eight-foot wall and hustled away. They were pursued by the Germans, and after running to the point of exhaustion were forced to climb trees, where they remained while the Germans searched below. Lieutenant Floyd was at large for five days, and finally became lost in the swampy country and

---

★The descriptions of the incident regarding Major Brown and the landing of six Breguet bombers in Germany are conflicting. It is said that all six aircraft ran out of fuel and landed intact, their crews being captured, but in Lieutenant Codman's escape report, he says that there were seven aircraft of which three were shot down and the remaining four crash-landed.

was captured at Erding on 15 September. He spent twenty-one days in solitary confinement, and for singing 'God help Kaiser Bill' with his comrades he got three extra days.

Regarding his treatment, he said he had two books to read which were in the Red Cross package. Except when Red Cross food was received, their two meals a day were insufficient for nourishment as it was cold and damp in the stone jail. For the escape he said they used a German magnetic razor with which they magnetised needles for the entire group to be used in place of compasses when any one of them wanted to escape.

1st Lieutenant Elihu H. Kelton, USAS. 185th Pursuit Squadron

On 30 October 1918, at about four o'clock in the afternoon, I left the 185th Aero Squadron at Rembercourt (1st Pursuit Group) in a Sopwith Camel (No. 13) for the purpose of shooting down a balloon at Villers-davant-Dun. I arrived at the lines and patrolled until nearly dusk, searching for German biplane machines. I then headed for the balloon, but about ten kilometres over the lines I saw a Fokker about 600 metres away, and five more in the distance. I attacked, and in the fight my motor quit. The Fokker shot up my machine on the way down so I landed out of control.

When I came to, there was a crowd of Huns around, two of whom were eagerly demanding in English when I thought the war would be finished. I was asked if I had any papers or arms but was not searched. They treated me very decently, giving me a cup of wine and cigarettes. In fact, the only expression of anger was by the pilot who shot me down. He seemed intensely peeved at first because I had spoiled his motor and forced him to land. He asked why I had attacked him.

That evening I was taken to several different headquarters where I was asked a few perfunctory questions which I did not answer. I walked to Wiseppa, from where I was taken to Stenay in

an auto. At Stenay a captain of the German Intelligence Force gave me a very thorough cross-examination. I stayed at Stenay overnight.

On the afternoon of 1 November, I was taken to Montmédy and put into a fair little prison camp which, however, we had to evacuate the next day on account of the Americans shelling a bridge nearby. In this camp a French 2nd lieutenant was put in with us, but the two Frenchmen who were with us immediately suspected him and told us he was a stool pigeon, so we were careful of our talk.

The next morning we were taken to the fortress on Montmédy where we stayed until 6 November. This room was full of cooties and fleas and we had very few blankets and very little wood. The food was always the same: roasted barley coffee and a day's ration of sour black bread for breakfast, cabbage soup for dinner, and more coffee and some uneatable vegetable jam for supper. On 3 November the adjutant of a German squadron invited us to tea. He was very cordial and asked no questions. His main object seemed to be to dispel our idea that Germans were Huns, Boche or barbarians, although doubtless he was on the watch for any information we might drop. As far as personal treatment was concerned I have no complaint to make. My combination flying suit was the only thing taken away.

On 6 November we started for Karlsruhe – four American officers under charge of two guards. We arrived at Karlsruhe on 7 November and were kept in a bare hotel room two nights and a day. On 9 November we were questioned at the hotel by a man who was very stupid. Then we were taken to the prison camp in town. Here our Sam Browne belts were taken away, but we received an issue of clothing, toilet articles and food from the American Red Cross. We lived almost entirely on the Red Cross food.

The signing of the Armistice was marked with great celebration in the city, and for some days rioting was feared. On the 18th we were allowed to go about the town under guard. On the 20th, as we could see no immediate chance of release, 1st Lieutenant Richard Aldworth (213th Pursuit Squadron), 1st Lieutenant William G. Caxton (41 Squadron RAF) and myself slipped the guard, and as soon as evening set in we left town. We crossed the Rhine and walked until we reached Lauterberg, the first town in Alsace, at four a.m. We never had any serious difficulties. From Lauterberg we hired carriages as far as Strasbourg, which we reached on 22 November. Every town in Alsace seemed very enthusiastically French. General Mitchell supplied us with funds and gave us permission to stay in Strasbourg a short time. We left by the first train to leave Strasbourg for Nancy (30 November). I rejoined my squadron and was reassigned two or three days later. I was paid sixty marks by the German government (in canteen money).

2nd Lieutenant David C. Beebe, USAS. 50th Observation Squadron

On 4 November at 1.45 p.m. Lieutenant D.C. Beebe, pilot, and 1st Lieutenant M.F. Lockwood, observer, of the 50th Squadron, 1st Observation Group, left the Clermont en Argonne Aerodrome in a Liberty-motor DH.4 as one of the two machines forming protection for a third doing a contact patrol mission for the 77th Division. At this time the American forces were advancing so rapidly that the location of the first lines was unknown, even approximately, and this mission was instructed to cover a large area.

The formation of three machines passed Buzancy, where no sign of activity was evident, and proceeded north to Le Chesne at an altitude of 500 feet. For a short time they circled about a large dam near Le Chesne until a single Boche mounted on horseback was soon in the town indicating that they were over hostile territory and that the lines were to the south. The formation turned south-east and almost immediately the machine of Lts Beebe and Lockwood was hit by machine-gun fire, the engine stopping instantly. An attempt to resort to reserve gas availed nothing. At this moment the Hun trenches had not been observed by the mission. There was only one available field to be reached from this limited altitude, which was then about 200 feet, and this field extended from east to west; to the south were poles and fences. As the machine glided into the field both pilot and observer saw that they were landing parallel to the line of trenches. Though it was landing, the machine-gun fire continued, hitting the machine incessantly. As these were new positions and little artillery bombardment had taken place, the ground was not broken up extensively, permitting the disabled machine to land without crashing thirty yards in front of the trenches. No friendly troops were in sight to the south. Machine-gun fire did not cease except in the pit opposite the machine.

Pilot and observer jumped out of the machine and hesitated for a moment, but fire continued, and then at the command of a Hun in the nearest pit the Germans emerged. No violence was displayed, but they were held in the pit until the other two machines circling above disappeared. The position comprised disconnected machine-gun pits. At the command pilot and observer crawled to a neighbouring pit and were led to an officer who, in French, requested identity cards. He inspected them and returned them.

From there they were led down the road and through the town of Tannay where a Hun soldier made a rush on them with an axe but was pushed away by the guard. At Regimental Headquarters considerable questioning was carried out, principally with regard to the attack of the next day. From here they were led to Brigade HQ, and then along the Aisne to the HQ of the 3rd Army Intelligence Department, arriving about 1.30 a.m. At this place, an *Oberleutnant* Brewer conducted the questioning in the presence of a stenographer who took down all that was said by the prisoners, who were separately questioned until 4.30 a.m. At 5.45 a.m. the captives were taken to the station where they joined another group of prisoners – an American lieutenant named Tiffany and four French officers – and boarded a train for Carignan.

Neither of the prisoners had overcoats, nor were they supplied with blankets during the trip to Libramont, which was the new HQ for the retreating 3rd Army. What food they had was furnished by civilians. At Libramont this party of officers were the only officers present. They were questioned in a small room on the second storey of a school house. In a large room on the first floor approximately eighty enlisted men – about forty Americans from the 77th Division, the remainder French. Neither officers nor enlisted men were supplied with blankets, but slept on board frames. The food consisted of soup in the middle of the day and barley coffee in the morning and at night. Almost daily questioning was conducted by *Oberleutnant* Brewer, who said he had been a platinum manufacturer in Newark, New Jersey, for fourteen years. Often Hun fliers were present. On the day before departure a few blankets were given to the officers, and a Hun army sergeant by the name of Ewald, who was formerly of New York, arranged to have food sent to the officer prisoners once a day from a hotel in town.

The Armistice came and all the prisoners were to be moved to a camp near Bouillon. A sergeant marched the party the thirty kilometres, and they were told they were to be held for two weeks more. The officers and many men succeeded in making their escape that night. The officers met outside Bouillon and one of the party, a French captain, managed to get up to a castle above the town. The German guards searched all night for the party, but in vain. The following day they marched all night to Sedan, though stopped several times, but those not directly concerned with prisoners were too occupied to know what to do with them.

Sedan and the French outposts were reached by noon on 14 November, and from there they were conducted by an American

party back to Clermont, and on the following day reported to the 1st Army HQ at Souilly. The officers were never searched, but asked to show contents of pockets, and no souvenirs were collected from their persons. *Oberleutnant* Brewer kept the prisoners' identity cards. Many of the guards who had been in America expressed their intention of returning after affairs were settled.

1st Lieutenant Brooke Edwards, USAS. 20th Bombardment Squadron

On 5 November 1918, the 20th Squadron made a bombing raid on Mouzom. Due to a strong south-westerly the formation of eight Liberty-motored de Havilland 4s was blown far into German territory after the bombs were dropped. On the way back to the lines we were attacked by three patrols of German aircraft. We drove off the first patrol (Fokker D.7s with blue markings with white crosses); the second patrol brought down one of our planes in flames, and the motor of the plane in which Lt Edwards (pilot) and Lt Payne (observer) were flying was crippled by machine-gun fire, and fell behind the formation; when the third patrol attacked us, we were practically alone. The markings of the Fokkers of this patrol were black and white stripes. They ripped out our gas tank by machine-gun fire, and wounded Lieutenant Payne in the left arm, disabling him. The ammunition for his twin Lewis gun was almost exhausted. He turned to tell the pilot what the conditions were in the rear seat, when an explosive bullet struck the breech of the Marlin gun close to the pilot's head. He thought the pilot wounded and took control, putting the plane into a steep nose dive. Three Fokkers followed, firing all the time, as the plane was still headed towards the American lines. It was necessary for the pilot to manoeuvre continually, and as the motor was barely turning over, the plane rapidly lost altitude. When we were very low, and close to the American lines, an enemy plane closed in on us and we shot him down. This was the second enemy plane we had shot down in combat.

Due to the crippled motor and the manoeuvring necessary to escape the pursuing Fokkers, and to the strong wind ahead, we were unable to reach our lines and landed in the lines of the *Württemburger Jaeger*. A private rushed at the pilot and presented a Luger at his head while others grinned. A *feldwebel*, however, ordered him back, saluted, and requested any papers we might have. We had no papers except a leave to Nice and a permission to use explosive bullets. We were able to destroy this later, however, before the Germans found it. We were taken to a field dressing station where Lieutenant Payne's wound was well and quickly dressed, and anti-tetanus injected. From there we were taken by an artillery officer, who later placed us on the *caissons* of his regiment and turned us over to the HQ at Louppy aur L'Gison, where we arrived on the night of 5 November.

We spent the night in the orderly room, and were not fed until noon the next day, when we received some soup and bread with Lieutenant Henry Brown, who had been shot down that morning by Fokkers. We were taken that afternoon to Virton, where a German intelligence officer gave us tea but didn't question us very closely, as he already knew of the Armistice. He showed us, however, excellent pictures of American aerodromes, and surprised us with his knowledge of the First Day Bombardment Group. We were kept in a room at Virton for three nights and two days. The food was neither good nor plentiful.

On 9 November two guards took us to Karlsruhe by train, and we arrived the next morning. As we arrived, revolutionaries with red bands on their arms were disarming all incoming troops. We spent the day and night in a room at the Europa Hotel at Karlsruhe, and the next morning we were taken to the permanent camp. Here we were given American Red Cross parcels, good barracks, a French orderly and every consideration that could be expected.

At 9.10 p.m. on the 20th, seven English officers and four Americans – Lts Brown, Fulton, Payne and Edwards – escaped from the camp by bribing a guard, stole a skiff from the Rhine bank, and landed at about one a.m. ten miles north of Lauterberg. We walked to a small village some four miles south of Lauterberg, rested there, and reached Selz on the night of the 21st. The Mayor of Selz showed us the greatest hospitality, free of any charge whatsoever. We reached Strasbourg on the night of the 22nd, and finally were able to get to Nancy by motor, reporting to Captain Zinn at Colombey-les-Belles.

2nd Lieutenant D.D. Watson, USAS. (observer)

Returning from a reconnaissance and bombing mission in the Lorraine sector on the evening of 7 November 1918, I was injured in the head by anti-aircraft fire. I was unconscious for a while, exact time unknown, but at 6.15 p.m. Allied time green rockets were fired and landing lights shown. We had requested landing flares be shown on our return, but did not think it was our field. It was very dark and misty and a strong south-westerly wind had blown us further in than we reckoned.

My pilot, 2nd Lieutenant Clark Robinson, attempted to land with weakened or shot controls and smashed into and through the German mechanics holding flares, landing upside down at the foot of a small hill. Both of us were pinned under the wreckage. When the Germans pulled us out they carried us to the officers' quarters, where my head was dressed. They then searched Lt Robinson and questioned us both, but made no threats over our refusal to talk. We had dinner with them which consisted of brown bread, roast beef, potatoes and dessert – some kind of pie. There was wine and beer, but we were not pressed to drink. After dinner our flying clothes were taken from us and German overcoats given instead. They were not very clean, but very warm. We were then carried to a guard house where we spent the night on wooden bunks.

Next morning, after dressing my wounds, we were carried to a railroad station at Bensdorf, and by train to Ranlach, where I was put in a hospital and Lt Robinson carried away under guard. The amenities were rather poor at this hospital, but I was treated kindly. I remained here until the morning of 10 November, when I was sent to Saargunen. I escaped from an ambulance there and went south on a freight train and crossed the lines south of Chateau Salines, coming into the French lines at Arrancourt on the morning of the 12th at daybreak.

From my limited experience and observations, food was comparatively scarce, the train service good, and discipline of the German Army excellent. We were given good treatment and no insults were offered by either civilians or soldiers.

2nd Lieutenant Clark Robinson (pilot), USAS. 8th Aero Squadron

Controls weakened, and Lieutenant D.D. Watson wounded in the head by archie fire after dark, 5.30 p.m. (Allied time), 7 November, while returning from reconnaissance of the sector, and bombing archie batteries south of Metz with twenty-four pound Cooper bombs. A mist had covered the river and there was a strong wind from the south-west. The plane was still in control and I headed south-west until 6.15. At 6.15 green rockets were fired to our left and landing lights shown.

I did not think that it was our field, though I had asked for landing lights in case I got back after dark. The night was very dark; there was no moon. I thought we had crossed the lines. I attempted to land with the lights, but when I throttled down the controls seemed to weaken. A number of German mechanics were holding flares to show us the limit of the field, and we accidentally ran into them. The plane landed upside down at the foot of a hill. We were both

pinned in and were pulled out by the Germans.

We were not mistreated. We were taken to the guardhouse where a doctor dressed Lieutenant Watson's wounds, and we were then taken to the officer's house and were given a good dinner with the officers. We were not pressed to drink and no questions were pressed. We had crashed at a Fokker field near Bensdorf.

We slept on bunks at the guardhouse, and the next day were sent by automobile and train, under guard, to Ranlach where Lieutenant Watson was put in hospital. I was sent to the prison camp at St Aveld. My treatment there was very good, though they had very little food.

At 7.00 p.m. on 11 November, thirteen French soldiers were sent back to France from the camp. I was dressed in a German overcoat and French helmet and had no difficulty leaving the camp with them. We were sent by train to Ouss and from there walked to Hinville.

1st Lieutenant B.B. Battle, USAS. 91st Observation Squadron

Shortly after noon on 12 June, Lieutenant Battle left his aerodrome in a Salmson plane to fly as protection for another Salmson which was to take pictures. The photographic mission was accomplished without incident, and the two machines were just crossing the lines on the return trip when Battle nosed his machine down and tried out his fixed gun. There was evidently some fault in the synchronisation, for at the first burst the propeller was shattered. Not having sufficient altitude to glide across the lines, he was forced to descend on the German side, landing between the first and second line of trenches. Bearing in mind that the first duty of a captured aviator is to destroy his machine, Battle endeavoured to set fire to his plane, but the men in the trenches opened fire on him and he was forced to desist. He held up his hands as token of surrender, but the fire continued, so he sought shelter in a shell hole. Here he was taken prisoner by an infantry officer of the Bavarian division occupying that sector.

Having landed just in front of the village of Flirey, the nearest German headquarters was at Thiacourt, and to this place Battle was marched. During the four days spent at Thiacourt, he was questioned on three different occasions but refused to talk. The intelligence officer finally lost patience and threatened that, unless certain questions were answered, a note would be dropped over the lines stating that 'An American pilot, Lieutenant Battle, has been killed in combat'. He was told to go ahead and drop the note. Shortly afterwards, an armament officer entered and asserted that incendiary bullets had been found in the belt of the Salmson's fixed gun. The intelligence officer then informed Battle that this was against the rules of warfare and that he would be shot unless he gave them all the information requested. This information was again refused.

Shortly afterwards, Lieutenant Battle was placed in a fourth-class coach and taken to Karlsruhe under the guard of an officer and three enlisted men. During the journey he asked to go to the toilet. This was granted, but the guard was watchful and caught him when he attempted to escape through the toilet window. On arrival at Karlsruhe, Battle was sent to the now famous Karlsruhe Hotel, which was fitted out with dictaphones. While here he fell ill but was refused a doctor. The food supplied to sick prisoners was the same as that given to those in good health: thin soup, barley coffee and black bread.

After nine days in this hotel he was sent to the camp for British aviators at Landshut, Bavaria. Here he was locked in a small unventilated room with twenty other officers. A short period of exercise was obtained each day in a small, filthy courtyard about twenty feet square. Food and living conditions were so bad that the officers requested in writing that they be moved to other quarters. After two weeks

this request was granted, and they were placed in an old castle nearby. The quarters at this place were better, and there was slight improvement in the food until ten days before their departure when Red Cross food was received. During his stay here Battle attempted to bribe a German sergeant-major to allow him to escape. This was reported, and the American was punished by being placed in solitary confinement for eight days.

Seven weeks after he arrived at the castle, Battle was removed to the prison camp at Villengen. The trip was made by train and took two days. During this time the prisoners were allowed to visit the latrine at eight-hour intervals only. Their shoes were removed to prevent attempts at escape. They received one meal during the trip. The camp at Villengen was reached on 14 September.

On the night of 6 October, the prisoners short-circuited the electric light wires of the camp and Battle, in company with four American and one French officer, made his escape by climbing over the fence. He was fired on by the guards but received nothing more serious than a bullet through his haversack. The six officers separated and each took a different route. Lieutenant Battle travelled for five nights through the Black Forest, hiding during the day. He met many people during the evenings, but they apparently supposed him to be some German wayfarer and he was only challenged twice. His food consisted of four pieces of hard tack a day. All went well until he reached the Rhine where he was captured by a police dog. He was immediately taken back to Villengen and put in solitary confinement for eighteen days.

At the end of this time he was told that he had been tried (his presence at the trial was evidently considered unnecessary) and convicted of inciting mutiny. For this offence he was sent to Fort Kurstein, a reprisal camp near Berlin. This place was never reached. At Cassel on 9 November, in the Grand Duchy of Hesse, the train was boarded by revolutionaries, among whom were a number of naval marines, and the guards were disarmed and the prisoners freed. Battle struck up an acquaintance with a marine who spoke English and who seemed very friendly. The two of them attempted to make their way to the Dutch border but were stopped by an officer, and the socialists who were in charge of the railway station ordered them back to Villengen. Lieutenant Battle talked to many of the revolutionaries and was told by all of them that the war was over and that he would be foolish to try and escape now as all prisoners would be released in a day or two. Discipline was very lax, and he believed that if he had had any money he could have reached Holland with little difficulty.

Boarding a train in company with his acquaintance the marine, Battle went to Frankfurt. Here he met a German officer and got on very good terms with him by giving him some Red Cross food. They went into the station bar together and had some drinks. Everyone was drinking and talking of the revolution, rejoicing that the Armistice was signed or soon would be. A statue of the Kaiser and pictures of Ludendorf and Hindenburg were torn down.

Leaving Frankfurt for Villengen, Battle tried to bribe the guard to take a route which would bring them close to the Swiss border. But the guard still possessed a strong respect for authority and wired ahead asking for reinforcements. When Villengen was reached a strongly armed guard was awaiting him and conducted him to the prison camp. It was necessary to remain in the camp until 25 November when nearly all the American prisoners were released. Lieutenant Battle went to Constance and remained there for three days, receiving excellent food. From there the journey was made across Switzerland and into France.

1st Lieutenant Marian Coldwell Cooper, USAS. 20th Bombardment Squadron

First Lieutenant Marian C. Cooper was assigned to the US Bombardment Squadron at Maulan, France, on 30 August 1918 as a pilot of a DH.4. One month later, on 26 September 1918, with his observer, Lt Edward Leonard, he was part of a seven-plane patrol on a bombing mission of Dun-sur-Meuse, and had just completed the mission and was turning for home when the aircraft was attacked by a squadron of Fokker fighters. In less than five minutes five of the bombers had been shot down, including Lt Cooper's. As his aircraft started to burn, Lt Cooper put the aircraft into a dive and then into a slide-slip to prevent the flames roasting him and his observer alive. His observer, Lt Leonard, had been hit in the neck by a bullet and was bleeding profusely, and Lt Cooper's hand and face were being burnt by the flames. The aircraft crash-landed and both crew members managed to extricate themselves from the wreckage. One of the Fokker pilots landed alongside the burning machine and accepted their surrender.

Troops soon arrived, and they were taken to a German field hospital and treated for their wounds. Later they were taken to another German hospital for further treatment, and then to a prisoner-of-war camp for the rest of the war. At the signing of the Armistice, they were released, and both returned to Paris, France.

Lt Cooper was assigned to duties in Paris with the US Air Service until July 1919, when Ignace Jan Paderewski, the Polish Premier, persuaded President Wilson to allow him to solicit volunteers from the US Air Service to help him form an air force and prevent the Bolshevik Army from invading Poland. Among the thirteen volunteers was Lt Marion C. Cooper, who with the others arrived in Warsaw in September 1919. The volunteers were inducted into the Koscisuzko Squadron, Marian Cooper being given the rank of major. The squadron was a mobile one and consisted of a train of railway coaches, flat cars and box cars for supplies and equipment, and as the area of action changed, so did the location of the squadron.

On 10 July 1920, Major Cooper was on patrol over the Bolshevik's front line when he came under heavy ground fire causing his engine to fail and forcing him to land. He was captured by the Bolsheviks and treated quite roughly as they did not take kindly to mercenaries being involved in their struggle. Taken to Moscow, Marian Cooper was put into a prisoner-of-war camp for the second time in his career, this time for nine months. He made his escape at the beginning of April 1921, and after travelling for twenty-six nights he crossed the Latvian border and into safety. Transportation was provided back to Warsaw, and at the end of May 1921 he returned to the United States.

His career after that is a matter of record. He became one of Hollywood's outstanding film producers with films such as *King Kong* and *Cinerama*. During the Second World War he joined the USAAC, finishing the war with the rank of brigadier-general.

Appendix 2:
Members of *L'Escadrille Lafayette* N. 124

Georges Thenault..18 April 1916–18 January 1918
Arnoux de Laage de Mieux.......................................18 April 1916–23 May 1917
Victor Chapman...18 April 1916–23 June 1916
Norman Prince...18 April 1916–15 October 1916
James R. McConnell...18 April 1916–19 March 1917
Kiffin Y. Rockwell..18 April 1916–23 September 1916
William Thaw..18 April 1916–18 February 1918
W. Bert Hall...18 April 1916–1 November 1916
Elliott C. Cowdin...18 April 1916–25 June 1916
Raoul Lufbery..24 May 1916–5 January 1918
H. Clyde Balsley...29 May 1916–18 June 1916
Charles C. Johnson...29 May 1916–31 October 1917
Lawrence Rumsey...4 June 1916–25 November 1916
Dudley L. Hill..9 June 1916–18 February 1918
Didier Masson..19 June 1916–8 October 1917
Paul Pavelka...11 August 1916–24 January 1917
Robert L. Rockwell...17 September 1916–18 February 1918
Frederick H. Prince..22 October 1916–15 February 1917
Robert Soubiran...22 October 1916–18 February 1918
Willis B. Havilland...22 October 1916–18 September 1917
Ronald Hoskier..11 December 1916–23 April 1917
Edmund C.C. Genet...19 January 1917–16 April 1917
Edwin C. Parsons...25 January 1917–26 February 1918
Stephen Bigelow...28 February 1917–11 September 1917
Edward F. Hinkle...1 March 1917–12 June 1917
Walter Lovell..31 March 1917–24 October 1917
Harold B. Willis...1 March 1917–18 August 1917
Kenneth Marr...29 March 1917–18 February 1918
William E. Dugan, Jr..30 March 1917–18 February 1918
Thomas M. Hewitt, Jr..30 March 1917–17 September 1917
Andrew C. Campbell, Jr...15 April 1917–1 October 1917
Ray C. Bridgman..1 May 1917–18 February 1918
Henry S. Jones...12 May 1917–18 February 1918
John A. Drexel..10 May 1917–15 June 1917
Charles H. Dolan II..12 May 1917–18 February 1918
Antoine de Maison-Rouge..28 May 1917–6 October 1917
James Norman Hall...16 June 1917–18 February 1918
Douglas MacMonagle..16 June 1917–24 September 1917
David McK. Peterson..1 June 1917–18 February 1918
James R. Doolittle..2 July 1917–17 July 1917
Louis Verdier-Fauvety...16 October 1917–18 February 1918
Christopher W. Ford...8 November 1917–18 February 1918

Appendix 3:
United States Squadrons in WWI

Fighter Squadrons
Escadrille Lafayette
L'Escadrille N. 471
13th Pursuit Squadron
17th Pursuit Squadron
22nd Pursuit Squadron
25th Pursuit Squadron
27th Pursuit Squadron
28th Pursuit Squadron
41st Pursuit Squadron
49th Pursuit Squadron
93rd Pursuit Squadron
94th Pursuit Squadron
95th Pursuit Squadron
103rd Pursuit Squadron
135th Pursuit Squadron
138th Pursuit Squadron
139th Pursuit Squadron
141st Pursuit Squadron
147th Pursuit Squadron
148th Pursuit Squadron
185th Pursuit Squadron
213th Pursuit Squadron
638th Pursuit Squadron

Bombardment Squadrons
11th Bombardment Squadron
20th Bombardment Squadron
96th Bombardment Squadron
100th Bombardment Squadron
155th Bombardment Squadron
163rd Bombardment Squadron
166th Bombardment Squadron

Marine Day Wing
Marine Squadron No. 7
Marine Squadron No. 8
Marine Squadron No. 9
Marine Squadron No. 10

Observation Squadrons
1st Observation Squadron
8th Observation Squadron
9th Observation Squadron
12th Observation Squadron
24th Observation Squadron
50th Observation Squadron
85th Observation Squadron
88th Observation Squadron
90th Observation Squadron
91st Observation Squadron
99th Observation Squadron
104th Observation Squadron
135th Observation Squadron
168th Observation Squadron
186th Observation Squadron
258th Observation Squadron
278th Observation Squadron
354th Observation Squadron

Balloon Companies
1st Balloon Company
2nd Balloon Company
3rd Balloon Company
4th Balloon Company
5th Balloon Company
6th Balloon Company
7th Balloon Company
8th Balloon Company
9th Balloon Company
10th Balloon Company
11th Balloon Company
12th Balloon Company
13th Balloon Company
14th Balloon Company
15th Balloon Company
16th Balloon Company
24th Balloon Company
25th Balloon Company
26th Balloon Company
42nd Balloon Company
43rd Balloon Company
44th Balloon Company
69th Balloon Company

Appendix 4:
Air Stations

Operational Royal Naval Air Stations (RNAS)
Anglesey, Wales
Bangor, Wales
Barrow-in-Furness (Walney Island), England
Bembridge Harbour, Isle of Wight, England
Calshot, Hants., England
Catfirth, Shetland Isles
Cattewater, Devon, England
Chickerell, Dorset, England
Cromarty, Scotland
Detling, Kent, England
Dover, Kent, England
Dundee, Scotland
Eastchurch, Isle of Sheppey, Kent, England
East Fortune, Scotland
Felixstowe, England
Fishguard, Pembrokeshire, Wales
Gosport, Hants., England
Grain & Port Victoria, Kent, England
Hornsea, Yorkshire, England
Houton Bay, Orkney Islands
Killingholme, Lincolnshire, England
Lee-on-Solent, Hants., England
Leuchars, Fife, Scotland
Manston, Kent, England
Mullion, Cornwall, England
Newhaven, Sussex, England
Newlyn, Cornwall, England
Owthorne, East Yorkshire, England
Padstowe, Cornwall, England
Portland, England

Redcar, North Yorkshire, England
Scapa, Orkney Islands
South Shields, Durham, England
Stonehenge, Wiltshire, England
Tresco, Isles of Scilly, England
Walmer, Kent, England
Westgate, England
Whitley Bay, Northumberland, England
Yarmouth, Norfolk, England

United States Naval Air Stations (USNAS)
USNAS Arcachon, France
USNAS Brest, France
USNAS Dunkirk, France
USNAS Fromentine, Italy
USNAS Ile Tudy, France
USNAS Killingholme, Britain
USNAS L'Aber Vrach, France
USNAS Le Croisic, France
USNAS Lough Foyle, Ireland
USNAS Porto Corsini, Italy
USNAS Queenstown, Ireland
USNAS St Trojan, France
USNAS Treguier, France
USNAS Wexford, Ireland
USNAS Whiddy Island, Ireland

United States Marine Corps Air Stations (USMCAS)
USMCAS La Fresne, France
USMCAS Ponta Delgada, Italy

Bibliography

A History of the Royal Air Force and United States Naval Air Service in Ireland, 1913–1923 (1988). Irish Air Letter, Dublin, Ireland.

Cooke, James J. (1996) *The US Air Service in the Great War: 1917–1919*. Westport, Connecticut: Praeger Publishers.

Emmons, Roger M. (1976) *US Marine Aviation in France, 1918*. Marine Corps Aviation Association.

Flammer, Philip M. (1981) *The Vivid Air*. The University of Georgia Press.

Hennessy, Juliette A. (1985) *The United States Army Air Arm – April 1861 to April 1917*. Washington DC: Office of Air Force History.

Jablonski, Edward (1964) *The Knighted Skies*. Thomas Nelson & Sons Ltd.

Knott, Captain Richard C., USN ret. (1997) *A Heritage of Wings*. Naval Institute Press.

Sloan, James J. (1994) *Wings of Honor*, Atglen, Pennsylvania: Schiffer Publishing.

Van Wyen, Adrian O. (1969) *Naval Aviation in World War One*. Washington DC: CNO.

Wise, S.F. (1986) *Canadian Airmen and the First World War*. Toronto University Press.

Woodhouse, Henry (1917) *Woodhouse's Text Book of Naval Aeronautics*. The Century Co.

Index